RAND CORPORATION

T0302507

Transforming Compliance

Emerging Paradigms for Boards, Management, Compliance Officers, and Government

Michael D. Greenberg

For more information on this publication, visit www.rand.org/t/cf322

Library of Congress Cataloging-in-Publication Data is available for this publication.

ISBN 978-0-8330-8767-6

Published by the RAND Corporation, Santa Monica, Calif.

© Copyright 2014 RAND Corporation

RAND® is a registered trademark.

Cover image: AdamRadosavljevic, iStock

Limited Print and Electronic Distribution Rights

This document and trademark(s) contained herein are protected by law. This representation of RAND intellectual property is provided for noncommercial use only. Unauthorized posting of this publication online is prohibited. Permission is given to duplicate this document for personal use only, as long as it is unaltered and complete. Permission is required from RAND to reproduce, or reuse in another form, any of its research documents for commercial use. For information on reprint and linking permissions, please visit www.rand.org/pubs/permissions.html.

The RAND Corporation is a research organization that develops solutions to public policy challenges to help make communities throughout the world safer and more secure, healthier and more prosperous. RAND is nonprofit, nonpartisan, and committed to the public interest.

RAND's publications do not necessarily reflect the opinions of its research clients and sponsors.

Support RAND

Make a tax-deductible charitable contribution at
www.rand.org/giving/contribute

www.rand.org

Preface

Recent decades have witnessed a tension between competing trends in corporate compliance activity. On the one hand, many companies have strengthened their compliance programs, and the officers who lead them, partly in response to standards established by the Federal Sentencing Guidelines. On the other hand, occurrences of workplace misconduct and fraud continue to present a serious problem for many private sector organizations. This fundamental tension is occurring against a backdrop of dramatic change in the landscape of corporate compliance and, by extension, that of organizational governance. The sources of this landscape change are varied, but among them are (1) the proliferation of new third-party contractual compliance obligations; (2) the professionalization of compliance practice as a discipline; (3) the increasing influence of government resolution agreements in driving corporate compliance efforts; and (4) the uncertain contours of privilege as applied to compliance programs and the compliance function. Taken together, these elements of landscape change suggest the possibility of an emerging paradigm shift in compliance. A series of questions follows. What would a new paradigm in compliance actually entail? What will boards, C-suites, and policymakers need to do to strengthen corporate compliance and integrity efforts going forward? What are the emerging risks that compliance programs are beginning to face, and how can the programs be improved to better address those risks? In turn, how will the role of the chief compliance officer shift and evolve, and what are the corresponding implications for the structure and resourcing of the compliance function?

On May 28, 2014, the RAND Corporation convened a symposium in Washington, D.C., to address these and related questions. Invited participants included senior thought leaders from the ranks of public company directors and executives, ethics and compliance officers, and stakeholders from government, academic, and nonprofit sectors. The symposium was the most recent in a series of annual RAND roundtable meetings focusing on topics in corporate compliance, governance, and ethics.

The current proceedings report summarizes key issues and topics from the May 28 symposium discussions. The document is not intended to be a transcript. Rather, it is organized by major theme and serves to highlight areas of agreement and disagreement among participants. With the exception of four invited papers that were written in advance and presented at the symposium, we do not attribute remarks to individual participants.

This report was funded with pooled resources from the RAND Center for Corporate Ethics and Governance, with additional support provided by New York Stock Exchange Governance Services, an Intercontinental Exchange company. These proceedings should be of interest to policymakers, regulators, corporate directors and executives, compliance and ethics practitioners, shareholders, nongovernmental organizations, and other stakeholders with interests in corporate governance, ethics, and compliance practices issues, both in the United States and abroad.

RAND Center for Corporate Ethics and Governance

The RAND Center for Corporate Ethics and Governance is committed to improving public understanding of corporate ethics, law, and governance and to identifying specific ways in which businesses can operate ethically, legally, and profitably. The center's work is supported by contributions from private-sector organizations and individuals with interests in research on these topics.

The center is part of the RAND Institute for Civil Justice, which is dedicated to improving the civil justice system by supplying policymakers and the public with rigorous, nonpartisan research. Its studies identify trends in litigation and inform policy choices concerning liability, compensation, regulation, risk management, and insurance.

Questions or comments about this report should be sent to the center director, Michael Greenberg (michael_greenberg@rand.org). For more information on the RAND Center for Corporate Ethics and Governance, see http://www.rand.org/jie/cceg or contact the director (cceg@rand.org).

Contents

Summary

Over the past six years, the RAND Corporation has organized a series of roundtable symposia on topics within corporate compliance, ethics, and governance. The symposia have brought together accomplished thought leaders across a range of professional backgrounds and perspectives to grapple with the challenges facing chief ethics and compliance officers (CECOs), boards, and senior management. Symposium topics have ranged from whistleblower protection, to the role of boards in compliance and ethics (C&E) oversight, to the unique challenges posed by C-suite–level compliance and misconduct. In all of these symposia, the aim has been to explore cutting-edge issues in compliance policy and practice, to identify exogenous factors affecting the compliance and governance landscape, and to elicit both diverse opinion and consensus across several stakeholder groups with interests in the landscape.

In May 2014, RAND undertook a forward-looking exercise during its annual symposium. The topic of this year's discussion involved the *transformation* of compliance, and the likelihood and potential implications of a qualitative shift in the compliance field over the coming decade. The symposium particularly focused on several change vectors currently operating on the compliance field, including (1) the proliferation of new third-party contractual compliance obligations; (2) the professionalization of compliance practice as a discipline; (3) the (contested) contours of privilege as applied to compliance programs and the compliance function; and (4) the increasing influence of government resolution agreements in driving corporate compliance efforts. Each of these vectors is associated with the potential for a transformational impact on the compliance field going forward. Collectively, they also serve as a point of departure for thinking about how the compliance obligation might shift in the future, how compliance practice and professionals might evolve in response, and how both descriptive and normative visions for the relationship between corporate board governance and the C&E function as a result.

It is within this context that RAND convened a roundtable meeting on May 28, 2014, entitled "Transforming Compliance: Emerging Paradigms for Boards, Management, Compliance Officers, and Government." The objective was to stimulate a forward-looking conversation about compliance as a field, factors that are likely to contribute to its transformational change, and practical implications for key stakeholder groups. The symposium brought together a group of two dozen senior thought leaders from the ranks of public company directors and executives, CECOs, and stakeholders from government, academic, and nonprofit sectors.

Prior to the symposium, several of the invited participants were asked to prepare and present formal remarks on selected transformational pressures now affecting the compliance field. The speakers presented their remarks during the first session of the symposium. Their white papers, distributed in advance of the event, offered a detailed perspective on each of the transformational vectors. The second and third sessions engaged the symposium participants in interactive discussions, launching from the foundational remarks initially offered by the authors of the white papers.

Several broad themes were touched on across the symposium discussions. The first was simply the recognition that compliance is a field in flux, and one that is undergoing change in several different ways at once. These include the sources of the compliance burden, the professional identity of compliance practitioners, and the posture of government enforcement efforts. All of these vectors are important to understanding how the field is likely to evolve in the future. Second, because CECOs and compliance programs operate in tandem with boards and senior executives, any transformation of compliance will also have an effect on boards and senior executives. To the extent that compliance programs (and CECOs) grow more effective within their companies, the burden of compliance risk for boards and C-suites will presumably be reduced. Contrariwise, to the extent that compliance becomes less effective, the burden of compliance risk for boards and C-suites will presumably be amplified. Third, our discussion of compliance transformation takes place in a broader corporate governance context, in which many large public companies and boards have identified reputation risk as a priority concern. Corporate reputation risk is at least partly tied to the compliance function, and to the risk of failure in compliance processes leading to crisis events. Thus, any discussion about the transformation of compliance invites reflection about business reputation risk and the future ability of the compliance function to help mitigate that risk.

Invited Remarks from Panelists

The symposium began with opening remarks offered by Michael Greenberg and Donna Boehme. These introductory remarks were followed by remarks from the authors of four invited white papers. The speakers were Scott Killingsworth, a partner with the law firm Bryan Cave LLP; Joseph Murphy, the director of public policy at the Society of Corporate Compliance and Ethics; Michael Volkov, CEO and owner of Volkov Law Group LLC; Peter Jaffe, CECO at the AES Corporation; and Michael Diamant, a partner at the law firm Gibson Dunn LLC. Their remarks were based on white papers titled "The Privatization of Compliance" (Killingsworth); "Compliance and Ethics as a Profession—In the Public Interest" (Murphy); "Redefining the Relationship of the General Counsel and Chief Compliance Officer" (Volkov); and "Learning the Hard Way: Ethics and Compliance Program Lessons Gleaned from Recent U.S. Resolution Agreements" (Jaffe and Diamant). The four papers were distributed to symposium participants in advance of the meeting to set the context and facilitate a dynamic discussion.

What Is the Emerging Paradigm for Compliance Programs of the Future, and What Are the Implications?

The second session of the symposium addressed each of the major vectors of change that were spotlighted in the symposium white papers: i.e., (1) the proliferation of new private-to-private (P2P) compliance obligations, (2) the professionalization of compliance practice as a discipline, (3) the contours of evidentiary privilege as applied to compliance programs and to the compliance function, and (4) the increasing influence of government resolution agreements in driving corporate compliance efforts. In each case, two questions were raised: How is this particular issue likely to affect compliance practice in the future? And how will compliance programs and the compliance function shift as a result? Secondary questions were raised concerning the impact of these transformational vectors on several other key stakeholder groups in the business community, apart from CECOs: most notably boards, senior executives and the C-suite, and government policymakers. Finally, the discussion touched on the notion of paradigm change itself, and what a new compliance paradigm might entail, or ought to entail, given the specific vectors of change that were spotlighted in the white papers.

Several of the comments in this session broadly spoke to the evolution of compliance as a field, and to the relevance of compliance to senior management more generally. One participant noted: "There is a big shift going on for the compliance function, in profile, seniority, independence, and seat at the table." Another participant suggested that "business risk and compliance risk are the same thing in today's marketplace." Still another observed:

> Reputation risk is a chief concern for many, many board members today. Directors know that they need to be worried about reputation, but they're often vague about what they specifically need to do. This involves a basic tieback to the compliance function, and to what the compliance officers are doing to address operational and strategic risk at the highest levels of their organizations.

In this vein, it was suggested that when corporate crisis events occur, they often involve law violations or ethical deficiencies that a robust and empowered compliance program might well have been able to prevent. On a related theme, another participant explained: "It [the compliance function] is for the public good." The discussion noted that an empowered CECO helps to safeguard both the reputation of the company and the public interest through the mitigation of compliance and corporate culture risks.

The symposium session included several other notable points of discussion among the participants:

- The source of the compliance obligation itself is shifting.
- Organizational culture will become even more important as a C&E focal point.
- Boards and senior executives may benefit from an independent compliance function in carrying out their own respective responsibilities.
- Effective compliance reflects a balance between transparency and confidentiality.
- Transformational trends in compliance are likely to affect and blend with each other.

- The empowered CECO is a foundational ingredient for the transformation of compliance.

How Can Boards, Management, Compliance Officers, and Government Respond in Support of More-Effective Compliance?

The final session of the symposium directly addressed several stakeholder groups that are likely to be affected by compliance transformation in the future: e.g., boards, C-suite executives, government policymakers, and compliance officers themselves. Symposium participants were asked what kinds of actions each of these stakeholder groups might take, either to move the compliance field in a positive direction or to respond to foreseeably changing conditions in compliance in a positive way? Some of the discussion focused on tangible things that CECOs, managers, and others could do differently on the ground in order to contribute to compliance transformation or to a better standard of compliance practice in the near future. Other points in the discussion focused on more normative considerations regarding the ideal structure and aim of compliance in the future, and the steps that various stakeholder groups might pursue in order to support those normative visions. Ultimately, the discussion circled back to two basic points. The first was the observation that transformational change in the compliance field is already well under way, partly in connection with the specific vectors discussed in the symposium white papers (e.g., the P2P trend, professionalization, and the debate over privilege). In one sense, then, the question for stakeholders is not whether the compliance field is likely to shift to a new paradigm in the future, but rather how the shift can be influenced in a maximally productive and useful direction. Second, the symposium discussion returned to the idea that boards and senior executives have become increasingly concerned with managing reputation risk for their companies, and that the evolution of compliance is occurring within a broader landscape of corporate governance that is also shifting. For boards and executives in particular, the transformation of compliance invites some reflection on the nature of corporate reputation risk and the potential for compliance programs and CECOs to serve as a useful asset in analyzing and responding to that risk.

The discussion in this session touched on several other major focal points:

- Boards can take steps to strengthen C&E capability and monitoring efforts.
- Management can focus on both structure and culture in the organization.
- Government can help by setting consistent standards and leading by example.
- Compliance officers can strengthen the field through improved efforts on role definition, professional development, education, and communication.

Acknowledgments

I wish to thank the panelists, speakers, and all those who participated in the roundtable discussions, without whom the exchange of ideas documented in these proceedings would not have been possible. I would also like to thank our event sponsor, New York Stock Exchange Governance Services, an Intercontinental Exchange company, for its generous support of this symposium event.

I would particularly like to acknowledge the invited authors and speakers at the symposium: Scott Killingsworth, Joseph Murphy, Michael Volkov, Peter Jaffe, and Michael Diamant. Ann Korologos and Justice Jack B. Jacobs both made notable contributions to the conversation, particularly in helping to open the discussion during the symposium sessions. A full list of participants and their affiliations can be found in Appendix B. My symposium cochair, Donna C. Boehme, provided invaluable contributions in structuring and facilitating the discussions, and in helping to bring the right group of people together around the conference table.

Finally, I would also like to thank Jamie Morikawa, Catherine Cruz, and Sarah Hauer at RAND for their assistance in organizing the symposium, managing logistics, capturing the discussions on the day of the event, and generating these proceedings.

Abbreviations

ADM	Archer Daniels Midland
C&E	compliance and ethics
CCEG	Center for Corporate Ethics and Governance
CCEP	Certified Compliance & Ethics Professional
CCO	chief compliance officer
CECO	chief ethics and compliance officer
COBC	Code of Business Conduct
CSR	Corporate Social Responsibility
DOJ	U.S. Department of Justice
FCPA	Foreign Corrupt Practices Act
GC	general counsel
HHS	U.S. Department of Health and Human Services
ICC	International Chamber of Commerce
J&J	Johnson & Johnson
OECD	Organisation for Economic Co-operation and Development
P2P	private to private
SCCE	Society of Corporate Compliance and Ethics
SEC	U.S. Securities and Exchange Commission

1. Introduction

Recent decades have witnessed a notable trend in corporate compliance and governance oversight. Many companies have made considerable progress in strengthening their corporate compliance programs. That progress has been achieved, in part, in response to the Federal Sentencing Guidelines. Originally (going back to 1991), the guidelines codified the basic elements for an effective compliance program. More recently, in 2004 and 2010, the guidelines added a new focus on ethical culture, board oversight, and independent compliance reporting, as they are key elements for achieving effective compliance and responsible corporate behavior. In the wake of these and other policy developments, compliance programs, and the chief ethics and compliance officers (CECOs) who helm them, have gained in visibility and prominence. The voice of the CECO is increasingly being heard at board and C-suite levels, in part as the tactical head of an empowered compliance effort, and also as a focal point for building an ethical culture within the corporation. Both the importance and the mechanics of effective compliance are gradually becoming better understood, not just by CECOs but also by the boards and senior executives who depend on them.

Over the past six years, the RAND Corporation has organized a series of roundtable symposia, with the aim of exploring the intersection of compliance and governance, the exogenous factors that help to shape them, and related policy. The symposia have brought together accomplished thought leaders across a range of professional backgrounds and perspectives to grapple with new challenges and opportunities facing CECOs, boards, and senior management. Some of the topics covered have included the role of corporate directors in compliance oversight, the implications of internal and external whistle-blowers for compliance risk, the multifaceted relationship between organizational culture and compliance, and the unique difficulties associated with C-suite–level ethical lapses and compliance problems.[1] Across these varied topic areas, several common themes have been raised by participants. Effective compliance involves more than the mechanical parsing of legal rules. An empowered and independent CECO is a basic element in any effective compliance program, and a key resource

---

[1] See Michael D. Greenberg, *Culture, Compliance, and the C-Suite: How Executives, Boards, and Policymakers Can Better Safeguard Against Misconduct at the Top*, Santa Monica, Calif.: RAND Corporation, CF-316-CCEG, 2013; Michael D. Greenberg, *Corporate Culture and Ethical Leadership Under the Federal Sentencing Guidelines: What Should Boards, Management, and Policymakers Do Now?* Santa Monica, Calif.: RAND Corporation, CF-305-CCEG, 2012; Michael D. Greenberg, *For Whom the Whistle Blows: Advancing Corporate Compliance and Integrity Efforts in the Era of Dodd-Frank*, Santa Monica, Calif.: RAND Corporation, CF-290-CCEG, 2011; Michael D. Greenberg, *Directors as Guardians of Compliance and Ethics Within the Corporate Citadel: What the Policy Community Should Know*, Santa Monica, Calif.: RAND Corporation, CF-277-CCEG, 2010; Michael D. Greenberg, *Perspectives of Chief Ethics and Compliance Officers on the Detection and Prevention of Corporate Misdeeds: What the Policy Community Should Know*, Santa Monica, Calif.: RAND Corporation, CF-258-RC, 2009.

for boards in carrying out their oversight responsibilities. Strong compliance programs tend to involve a mix of both hard and soft elements—modifying the structure and control processes within firms, as well as seeking to promote culture changes. In addition, compliance tends to work best when companies and their managers are walking the walk, as well as talking the talk: i.e., when there is no inconsistency between values and behavior, between internal and external messaging, and between the tone at the-top and the controls and everyday practices throughout an organization.

In May 2014, RAND undertook a forward-looking exercise in its annual compliance symposium. The topic this year involved the transformation of compliance and the likelihood of a paradigm shift in the field over the coming decade. A basic threshold question follows: What does *transformation* or *paradigm shift* actually mean in this context? The idea that we're trying to get at is qualitative change, such that future practice may depart from historical practice, not solely in degree but in kind. Transformation in this sense is a descriptive concept. When changes in the business landscape and in policy lead to a new and fundamentally different set of operational and risk problems, then a transformation in compliance may become the inevitable and necessary response. At least in principle, this is something that can be observed over time. *Transformation* is also a normative concept. Given the new challenges now facing compliance, how *should* the field change going forward in order more effectively to serve both business and the public interest? The aim of the RAND symposium was to grapple with both of these perspectives on transformation, in the context of several identified vectors that are currently pressing the compliance field to change. Whether any one of the vectors is truly transformational in its own right is open to debate. But taken together, they invite reflection on where the compliance field is going in the future, on major leverage points that are likely to shape the field, and on competing visions for what the compliance function and profession ought to look like, and ought to achieve.

As of 2014, several (arguably) transformational factors are currently affecting compliance. Perhaps the most obvious is new technology. Ubiquitous outside scrutiny through social media, combined with executives now equipped with smartphones and round-the-clock access to email, suggests both heightened compliance risk and heightened expectation for swift management response to problems.[2] For this year's RAND symposium discussion, we chose to focus on several *other* nontechnology avenues of change now affecting compliance. The selected topics include (1) the proliferation of contractual—or private-to-private (P2P)—compliance obligations; (2) the debate over evidentiary privilege, the compliance function, and the relationship between compliance and the office of the general counsel (GC); (3) the movement

---

[2] Note that the impact of technological change on compliance responsibility, particularly at the C-suite level, was the topic of keynote remarks delivered in RAND's 2013 symposium roundtable event. See Ruben Castillo, "The Technology Challenge of the United States' Aggressive Compliance Environment," in Michael D. Greenberg, *Culture, Compliance, and the C-Suite: How Executives, Boards, and Policymakers Can Better Safeguard Against Misconduct at the Top*, pp. 33–38, Santa Monica, Calif.: RAND Corporation, CF-316-CCEG, 2013.

toward professionalization of compliance as a discipline; and (4) the increasing influence of government resolution agreements, and their substantive provisions, in helping to define the state of the art in compliance practice. Each of these topics reflects a different form of transformational pressure, flowing from a different part of the compliance landscape. Each is the subject of a white paper written for the symposium and reproduced in this report.[3] The white papers offer ample commentary on why each of the vectors is likely to be important, considered by itself. In practice, though, these vectors are operating concurrently, and in a mutually recursive way. Much of the discussion in the symposium involved trying to foresee some of the likely implications for the compliance field on the horizon. Ultimately, the lowest common denominator is simple: Change is coming.

Stepping back, our discussion of compliance transformation takes place at a time when executives and directors are themselves struggling with a shifting landscape. In recent years, many large public companies have acknowledged in their annual reports that reputation risk is material, and by extension, that the C-suite and board have an affirmative obligation to address this. There is far less consensus about the specific steps that leadership is supposed to take in order to manage reputation risk. Three things seem clear. The first is that high-value episodes of corporate fraud, and of executive moral turpitude, can easily become reputational crisis events for large corporations. The second is that the role of the compliance function, and of the CECO, is to address exactly these sorts of events: to prevent them to the extent possible, and to respond and help limit the damage, when necessary. The third is that compliance is dedicated not just to ensuring obedience to legal rules but also to engineering an organizational culture in which high standards of behavior and integrity are shared. In an important sense, reputation is the outward reflection of an inner organizational culture: a set of expectations about how business will be done, and how all parties to the enterprise will be treated. Thus, the CECO is potentially a key asset both to the board and to senior leadership for responding to a set of reputational risks that may otherwise be nebulous and difficult to identify. Put another way, boards and top executives are under pressure to manage a new category of risk. The transformation of compliance is, in important part, a response to the same problem. An empowered CECO and a transformed compliance function have the potential to serve as a bulwark for safeguarding corporate culture and reputation.

It is within this context that RAND convened a roundtable symposium on May 28, 2014, entitled "Transforming Compliance: Emerging Paradigms for Boards, Management, Compliance Officers, and Government." The objective was to stimulate a forward-looking conversation about compliance as a field, factors that are likely to contribute to its transformational change, and practical implications for key stakeholder groups. The symposium brought together a group of two dozen senior thought leaders from the ranks of public company directors and executives, CECOs, and stakeholders from government, academic, and nonprofit sectors. The symposium

[3] See Chapter Two and Appendix C.

agenda can be found in Appendix A of these proceedings, and the full list of participants is provided in Appendix B.

Prior to the symposium, several of the invited participants were asked to prepare and present formal remarks on selected transformational pressures now affecting the compliance field. The speakers presented their remarks during the first session of the symposium. Chapter Two of these proceedings features a short summary of these remarks, and Appendix C includes the full text of the invited papers.

The second session of the symposium involved a moderated discussion on the emerging paradigm for compliance programs of the future and the broad implications that can be gleaned from transformative factors now operating on the field. Chapter Three summarizes the major themes and topics of conversation in that session.

The third and final session of the symposium involved a moderated discussion of related concerns and next steps from the varied perspective of boards, executives, CECOs, and policymakers. Chapter Four summarizes the major themes and ideas from that session.

2. Invited Remarks from Symposium Participants

The symposium began with opening remarks offered by Michael Greenberg and Donna Boehme. These introductory remarks were followed by invited remarks from several of the participants in attendance: Scott Killingsworth, a partner with the law firm Bryan Cave LLP; Joseph Murphy, the director of public policy at the Society of Corporate Compliance and Ethics; Michael Volkov, CEO and owner of Volkov Law Group LLC; Peter Jaffe, CECO at the AES Corporation; and Michael Diamant, a partner at the law firm Gibson Dunn LLC. Their remarks were based on invited white papers, which are reproduced in Appendix C of this report. Each author and topic brought an important expert viewpoint and helped set the context for the symposium discussion. This chapter presents a brief summary of each of the four white papers.

Summary: The Privatization of Compliance

Scott Killingsworth, Bryan Cave LLP

Companies face a new and growing array of compliance obligations imposed by their trading partners and counterparties, primarily via contracts and codes of conduct. In a sentence, compliance is becoming privatized, and privatization is going viral.

A Qualitative Shift in Compliance

New obligations for companies are arising through P2P relationships, in which contractual counterparties impose on each other new compliance burdens, new risks, and new liabilities and enforcement mechanisms. In context, companies and their compliance officers may find themselves ensnared in a web of P2P relationships, with sometimes-conflicting obligations. The P2P network context is reshaping the compliance function and raising new questions about who is answerable to whom, both internally and across company boundaries.

Is the Trend Moving in a Positive Direction?

The trend toward P2P compliance signals that enterprises across the value chain share in each other's compliance risks and can benefit from each other's compliance activity. Some aspects of the P2P trend are consensual and reflect best practices in compliance and accepted principles of corporate responsibility. Other facets of the trend may threaten to impose idiosyncratic and granular P2P compliance obligations on companies, in ways that can sometimes be suboptimal, deleterious, or even self-sabotaging.

Origins and Protagonists

The trend toward P2P compliance finds its roots in government enforcement and procurement activity, in the human rights and corporate social responsibility (CSR) movement, and in the corporate response to the disaggregation of the supply chain. Government enforcement and procurement have generated high-profile test cases concerning third-party liability for compliance failures. The human rights and CSR movement has contributed a complementary set of trickle-down compliance standards and enforcement mechanisms driven by multinational NGOs and advocacy campaigns. And the corporate response to supply chain disaggregation (and to other forms of risk shifting) has resulted in improved monitoring of counterparty compliance risk in recognition of increasing third-party risk exposure.

Codes, Contracts, and Consequences

P2P compliance obligations are being imposed contractually. Such obligations take many forms, including procedural and substantive rules, enforcement and monitoring provisions, damages and remedy provisions, and cascading "downstream" requirements for business associates.

Needless to say, neither P2P contracts nor P2P codes are uniform. Consequently, there is significant potential for mischief associated with idiosyncratic drafting, ambiguous provisions, and the interaction between code provisions and contract requirements. One important implication is that business contracts that refer to P2P codes may make the latter enforceable by private rights of action under contract. This could sometimes have perverse consequences for corporate counterparties. More broadly, P2P contracting could also lead to a broader proliferation of impractical or unfair P2P compliance obligations, particularly in a world of unequal bargaining power, and in a world where careless or predatory drafting of P2P compliance provisions is commonplace.

The Compliance Officer's Dilemma

P2P obligations present a series of potential mismatches and hazards for companies, particularly in seeking to reconcile the tension between operational goals and compliance priorities. Even the process for vetting and negotiating new P2P provisions in business contracts can place compliance officers in an odd position in assessing whether outside contractual demands would impose an unreasonable compliance burden for a company to actually carry out.

Managing P2P compliance responsibly requires a protocol for handling both incoming P2P demands and the company's own P2P requests of third parties. The process should include elements of triage; the cataloging of standard acceptable and unacceptable contract provisions; triggers for escalated review (such as indemnity clauses); identification of the stakes, including applicable contractual remedies, in each P2P provision; and so on. Critical to this process is clarity—in advance—as to the authority and reporting lines of the compliance officers who are going to be involved in P2P review and triage.

Childhood's End: Toward a Mature P2P Compliance Regime

The corporate community has a collective stake in simplifying management of the P2P compliance process while fostering accountability throughout the value chain. In general, those companies least vulnerable to unfair P2P pressures, and most able to inflict them, are the largest and most powerful enterprises. These should accept a leadership role in an effort to rationalize P2P standards. Many such companies have already done so.

Ultimately, the broader goal for the corporate community should be to establish common P2P expectations that are proportional, balanced, and sensitive to the particular risk profile of any given relationship. Assuming the right consensus within the business community, this kind of paradigm shift around P2P compliance can and should be achieved.

Summary: Compliance and Ethics as a Profession—In the Public Interest

Joseph Murphy, Society for Corporate Compliance and Ethics

The field of compliance and ethics (C&E) is dedicated to preventing and detecting misconduct within organizations. Although relatively new, the field is becoming increasingly professionalized. This invites important questions for the future.

What Is the Field of C&E, and Who Is in It?

Because the C&E function entails a range of management tools to prevent and detect misconduct, C&E practitioners represent an equally broad set of skills and competencies. Effective compliance programs include many elements, among them risk assessment, standard setting, internal controls, effective communications, meaningful discipline, appropriate incentives, audits and monitoring, and reporting and investigation mechanisms. Consonant with the foregoing, the types of positions in the C&E field are also broad and multidisciplinary. What all C&E practitioners share in common is a mission and an ethical commitment. While practitioners in this field have an employer, they also have a singular duty to protect the public, operating in an environment where they may be the first to know of incipient harm. Unlike others within their organizations, this is not a sideshow of their job; this is their entire job.

What Does It Mean to Call C&E a "Profession"?

In general, the traditional professions (e.g., law, medicine) tend to have several elements in common. Among them are specialized knowledge and training, the organization of professional societies, disciplinary self-regulation, autonomy from other vocational groups, identification of members with the shared experience of their professional colleagues, and commitment to a well-defined public interest. The C&E field already meets most of these criteria, and it is evolving in ways that will likely enhance its professional stature in the future. Among the indicia of the traditional professions, the one element not yet pinned down for the C&E field is the role of government in supporting and endorsing C&E professional self-regulation, standard setting, and disciplinary mechanisms. It remains to be seen whether, and how, government ought to play a more formal role in backing C&E as a profession, as through the certification of practitioners.

The Public Interest and the Need for Professionalism

Perhaps the most important point of commonality between medicine and law is their connection to the public interest. All citizens face the prospect of dealing with medical and legal emergencies, in which personal well-being depends on the quality and integrity of somebody else's professional service. In consequence, society has a genuine interest in ensuring that such professionals are indeed committed, competent, and conscientious in the performance of their duty.

The argument can be made that society has an even stronger public interest in the competency and mission of C&E practitioners. When professional standards are violated in law and medicine, the consequential harm tends to fall on individual patients in hospitals or clients in court cases. By contrast, when C&E violations occur in major companies, there is the potential for dramatic negative consequences with more widespread impact (e.g., the Bhopal disaster, Enron debacle, BP oil spill).

Organizational misconduct can result in high-stakes harm to society, and history suggests that established forms of government oversight have often been ineffective in controlling and preventing such misconduct. Taken together, these circumstances make a strong case for professionalizing C&E as a discipline.

How a Strong Professional Ethical Standard Can Empower C&E

One of the important ways that professional status can empower C&E practitioners is by instituting professional and ethical standards that help to trump management short-term interest. To the extent that C&E practitioners have formal standards of conduct, codified and enforced under binding ethics rules, the profession itself is elevated to stand explicitly behind the practitioner when inevitable conflicts arise with management.

Under existing Society of Corporate Compliance and Ethics (SCCE) ethics rules, C&E practitioners are obligated to intervene when management is otherwise charting an unethical or improper course. Sometimes, the role of the compliance officer is to say "no" to senior management, when "no" is an answer that senior management does not want to hear. Stronger professional status and more external support could help C&E practitioners to be more successful in playing this kind of role.

Going Forward

There is a range of steps that can be taken to support further professionalization of C&E as a discipline. For practitioners, more effort can be put into promoting ethical and professional codes, and then incorporating them by reference into corporate policy and employment practices more broadly. Additional steps could be taken to build more formal professional education opportunities focused on the code of professional ethics. Complementary steps could be taken by government, and by large organizations, to reinforce and strengthen the professional status of C&E along with adherence to their professional ethics codes.

If the field is ultimately to succeed in carrying out its public mission, and in protecting both corporations and society from misconduct, further steps toward professionalizing the C&E field are desirable, and perhaps inevitable.

Summary: Redefining the Relationship of the General Counsel and Chief Compliance Officer

Michael Volkov, The Volkov Law Group LLC

The past decade has witnessed a sea change in the positioning and responsibility of chief compliance officers (CCOs). CCOs are increasingly being elevated to assume more responsibility, to carry new burdens, and to embody greater independence within senior management. The trend toward CCO independence has notably met resistance, however, among some GCs, who either fear the potential for legal risk resulting from an independent compliance function or see the empowerment of the CCO as a diminution of their own sphere of influence. These concerns have crystalized in the context of the federal *Barko v Halliburton* case, now under appeal.[4] *Barko* superficially focuses on the foundation of attorney-client privilege, and on the application of privilege to compliance investigations within corporations. Substantively, though, the case heralds a deeper set of concerns: to wit, the evolving relationship between CCOs and GCs, the important nonlegal aspects of both roles, and the trade-off between confidentiality and transparency inherent in any corporate compliance program.

The Importance of Attorney-Client Privilege to Legal and Compliance Functions

The GC is the ultimate guardian of legal risks within a company, while the CCO builds on the company's legal compliance foundation, by promoting not only compliance with the law, but adherence to a culture of ethics and a specific business code of conduct. One of the GC's most important tools is the attorney-client privilege. It is the means by which the GC encourages frank discussion of legal issues, learns about potential legal problems, and gives effective legal advice.

The role of the CCO is different and complementary. An effective C&E program is designed to be open and transparent to employees, management and the government. Such a program depends on a balance between confidentiality and transparency. The CCO needs to be able to draw on the attorney-client privilege, and to coordinate closely with the GC, in investigating and responding to violations of law. But the CCO also needs to conduct many of his responsibilities outside the attorney-client privilege, as through audits, training, hot line monitoring, complaint investigation, ethics communications, etc. Transparency in these varied functions is a basic part of what helps to build a culture of compliance, and a deeper organizational commitment to honesty, fair dealing, and rule of law. Thus, blanket confidentiality, secrecy, and claims of privilege are antithetical to what compliance programs are fundamentally striving to achieve.

---

[4] *Barko v. Halliburton*, No. 1:05-cv-1276 (DDC Mar. 6, 2014). Note that following the date of the RAND symposium and the presentation of these remarks, the U.S. Court of Appeals for the DC Circuit overturned the judgment of the lower court and ruled that Halliburton's internal investigation fell within the scope of attorney-client privilege. See *In re: Kellogg, Brown & Root*, 2014 WL 2895939 (CADC June 27, 2014).

Drawing the Lines Between Compliance and Legal: Internal Investigations and the Attorney-Client Privilege

The boundary between the legal and compliance functions is tested in the handling of internal investigations. Every compliance program requires an internal investigation and discipline process to identify and respond to potential legal and code-of-conduct violations. In order to ensure that attorney-client privilege applies in appropriate instances, the internal investigation process needs to be closely coordinated with the legal department.

The recent *Barko* case highlights the subtlety of the challenges involved. The facts in *Barko* involve allegations of fraud and abuse within KBR in the context of the company's reconstruction activities in Iraq. Extensive KBR internal investigation and reporting activities were carried out, but these activities ignored the *Upjohn* requirements for establishing attorney-client privilege. The findings from KBR's investigations were ultimately kept secret from the public for many years. A federal district court in *Barko* recently concluded that KBR's internal investigation and reports are not privileged, as these were of a "business nature" and not undertaken for purposes of "giving legal advice." That district court finding is now on appeal and has been interpreted by some advocates as broadly threatening the viability of internal investigation activities undertaken by companies.

There are two basic flaws in this argument. The first is factual. In the facts of the *Barko* case, KBR conducted its own internal investigations without attention to attorney-client privilege and while ignoring the basic steps needed to ensure application of the privilege. Thus, the case is better understood as a tactical failure in KBR's investigation activity, rather than as a fundamental problem in the contours of attorney-client privilege.

The second flaw is deeper and conceptual. It is now being argued by KBR, and by various amicus curiae briefs, that effective compliance can only occur in the shelter of an expanded attorney-client privilege, and by extension, under the supervision of the GC. That argument moves in the opposite direction than the last two decades of federal enforcement policy on corporate compliance. The trend toward increasing independence for the compliance function, and for the CCO, follows from the premise that compliance is not narrowly aimed at minimizing legal risk, or at supporting the GC in giving legal advice. Instead, the compliance function is supposed to balance confidentiality and transparency. The compliance function is also supposed to balance proactive risk reduction through culture and behavior change, and reactive risk reduction in the wake of a material violation of the law.

Thus, the right way to think about optimizing the relationship between the CCO and the GC is through effective coordination between the two, in order to both protect the company against legal risk and achieve a culture of compliance that minimizes the likelihood of law violations in the first place.

The Way Forward for GCs and CCOs

Every company needs attorney-client privilege to facilitate internal communications on legal issues, and to ensure legal compliance. Such communications are critical to the GC's function, and they also ensure a company's compliance with the law. But how do we reconcile the role of the GC and the importance of attorney-client privilege with the CCO's obligation to carry out compliance activities with a presumption of transparency and disclosure?

The answer is that CCOs and GCs need to partner with each other and coordinate effectively in the context of investigations of law violation. When legal risk is recognized and legal advice needs to be given, then effective coordination between the two roles becomes crucially important. But equally important is forming a robust and empowered compliance function in the first place—one that is capable of supporting a genuine culture of integrity within the company. Broadly subordinating transparency to confidentiality, and compliance to legal, is unlikely to serve the latter aim.

Summary: Learning the Hard Way: C&E Lessons from Recent U.S. Resolution Agreements

Peter Jaffe, AES Corporation
Michael Diamant, Gibson Dunn

One important way that the government exerts influence on compliance involves resolution agreements, which decide the investigation of occurrences of corporate wrongdoing. Here we review recent trends from resolution agreements entered into by the Department of Justice (DOJ), the Securities and Exchange Commission (SEC), and the Department of Health and Human Services (HHS).

Lessons from Recent Settlements

Recent DOJ resolution agreements have specified a handful of requirements for an effective compliance program, including (1) high-level (management) commitment, (2) supporting policies and procedures, (3) periodic risk-based review, (4) proper oversight and independence for the compliance function, (5) effective compliance training and guidance, (6) robust internal reporting and investigation, (7) appropriate enforcement and discipline mechanisms, (8) risk-based due diligence on third-party relationships, (9) risk-based due diligence on mergers and acquisitions, and (10) compliance monitoring mechanisms and periodic testing.

Risk-Based Approaches to Compliance Have Become More Important But Raise Questions

As spotlighted by the recent joint DOJ-SEC resource guide on the Foreign Corrupt Practices Act (FCPA), many requirements in resolution agreements underscore the importance of an analytical, risk-based approach to compliance, particularly in identifying and prioritizing risks. Ambiguity remains in the details, however, such as in determining what the appropriate standard for risk tolerance is, and in whether compliance violations ex post will be viewed by the government as evidence of deficient compliance triage mechanisms ex ante. It remains to be seen how future resolution agreements will address these sorts of risk-assessment details with compliance.

Increasing Compliance Obligations Are Being Imposed on Boards and Managers

Some recent resolution agreements notably specify compliance requirements for boards and managers, including annual compliance certifications and training, more explicit responsibility for compliance oversight, and visible support for the compliance program. Assuming that the trend continues, then at least for those companies directly involved in regulatory resolutions, the result will be increased pressure for boards and management to play a more active role in compliance endeavors in the future.

Resolutions Place More Emphasis on Third-Party Due-Diligence Efforts

Several recent resolutions involve allegations of corporate misconduct involving third-party intermediaries, underscoring the importance of effective compliance due-diligence programs vetting outside business relationships partners. This concern plays a particularly central role in FCPA compliance (e.g., the 2013 Archer Daniels Midland case) but manifests in other contexts as well (e.g., the 2013 Johnson & Johnson case). If the current trend in enforcement resolutions continues, then government will likely press for more and stronger third-party due-diligence efforts in the future.

Compliance Training and Engagement Are Important Factors for Mitigating Risk

Recent resolutions suggest that CCOs who implement robust employee training and messaging initiatives may thereby inoculate their employers from rogue-actor liability, as demonstrated in the 2012 DOJ investigation of Morgan Stanley and Garth Peterson. When a company documents that extensive compliance training sessions and notices were actually given to the rogue actor, then that contributes to the strength of the compliance approach and may help to mitigate the risk of subsequent corporate liability and prosecution.

Resolution Agreements Are Pressing for the Empowerment and Reporting Access of the CCO

Two other important trends in resolution agreements have been to strengthen the position and autonomy of the CCO and to increase reporting access by the CCO to both senior executive and board levels. Specific resolution agreements and enforcement agencies have approached this issue in different ways, but the commonality across them is CCO empowerment, with enhanced reporting access between the CCO and the corporation's senior governing authority (i.e., the board).

Conclusion

In recent years, increasing government interest in corporate compliance has manifested itself through resolution agreements, which discharge civil and criminal investigations against corporate defendants. Resolutions exert influence on the business community both through the direct impact on defendants and as a broader source of guidance on compliance best practice, as seen through the eyes of the government. Going forward, companies can choose to learn from the compliance provisions included in resolution agreements and to draw on them for insight regarding what enforcement agencies are looking for when the they review the effectiveness of a compliance program.

3. What Is the Emerging Paradigm for Compliance Programs of the Future, and What Are the Implications?

The second session of the symposium addressed each of the major vectors of change that were spotlighted in the symposium white papers—i.e., (1) the proliferation of new third-party contractual compliance obligations; (2) the professionalization of compliance practice as a discipline; (3) the contours of evidentiary privilege as applied to compliance programs and to the compliance function; and (4) the increasing influence of government resolution agreements in driving corporate compliance efforts. In each case, the question was raised of how this particular issue will likely affect compliance practice in thc future, as well as how compliance programs and the compliance function will shift as a result. Secondary questions were raised concerning the impact of these transformational vectors on several other key stakeholder groups in the business community, apart from CECOs—most notably boards, senior executives and the C-suite, and government policymakers. Finally, the discussion touched on the notion of paradigm change itself, and what a new compliance paradigm is likely to entail, or ought to entail, given the specific vectors of change that were spotlighted in the white papers.

Several of the comments in this session broadly spoke to the evolution of compliance as a field and to the relevance of compliance to senior management more generally. One participant noted: "There is a big shift going on for the compliance function, in profile, seniority, independence, and seat at the table." Another suggested: "Business risk and compliance risk are the same thing in today's marketplace." Still another observed:

> Reputation risk is a chief concern for many, many board members today. Directors know that they need to be worried about reputation, but they're often vague about what they specifically need to do. This involves a basic tieback to the compliance function, and to what the compliance officers are doing to address operational and strategic risk at the highest levels of their organizations.

In this vein, it was suggested that when corporate crisis events occur, these often involve law violations or ethical deficiencies that a robust and empowered compliance program might well have been able to prevent. On a related theme, another participant observed: "It [the compliance function] is for the public good." The discussion noted that an empowered CECO helps to safeguard the reputation the company, as well as the public interest, through the mitigation of compliance and corporate culture risks.

The symposium session included several other notable points of discussion among the symposium participants:

- The source of the compliance obligation itself is shifting.
- Organizational culture will become even more important as a C&E focal point.
- Boards and senior executives depend on an independent compliance function in order to carry out their own respective responsibilities.
- Effective compliance reflects a balance between transparency and confidentiality.
- Transformational trends in compliance are likely to affect and blend with each other.
- The empowered CECO will be a foundational element in the transformation of compliance.

The Source of the Compliance Obligation Itself Is Shifting

One of the major themes of discussion involved P2P compliance, and the related transformational impact of shifting the compliance burden toward contractual obligations and moving beyond government regulation. Mixed opinions were expressed about whether this trend is likely to have a positive influence on the field over time. On the plus side, it was observed that P2P compliance pressures can result in a strong push for better behavior from contractual counterparties: "The message [of strong compliance] has to be delivered by vendors and sellers. . . . We don't want to work with you because you don't meet our standards." In a complementary vein, another person observed: "We are seeing the same issue come up in [the context of] supplier due diligence: If you implement a compliance program that meets our standards, [then] we will put you onto our preferred vendor list." Several other symposium participants expressed more concern about the possible ill effects associated with P2P compliance. One person said, "Contractual vendor provisions often involve similar, but not identical, language. The result is to throw sand into the gears of compliance." Another suggested that the primary ill effects of P2P compliance would be felt by companies lacking the negotiating power to push back against unreasonable contract provisions. Still another responded that "a lot of P2P compliance codes never leave the department where they land—so the judgment-rendering part of the company never sees them." It was noted that in the worst-case scenario, unreasonable or poorly drafted P2P obligations might be entered into by a company that simply neglects to conduct a thoughtful review—a chaotic and perverse result from the standpoint of effective compliance and risk reduction. Another symposium participant drew a connection between P2P and the professionalization of the C&E field and observed that P2P compliance pressures may exacerbate the tension between the CECO's autonomous role as corporate conscience and his or her operational role in imposing and responding to P2P requirements through the commercial contracting process (i.e., serving as an operational decisionmaker alongside procurement, business development, and/or sales personnel).

Ultimately, it was acknowledged that the future direction of P2P compliance might follow one of several radically different trajectories, and in that light, suggestions were debated for making P2P obligations more useful and less burdensome. One person recommended that the largest and most influential companies might be in the best position to develop a "neutral" set of

P2P compliance provisions, which might then be appropriate to codify and distribute more broadly. Another participant amplified this notion, arguing that P2P contractual provisions ought to focus on broad principles rather than on narrow details. It was suggested that the details might better be incorporated by reference to published codes, thereby sidestepping the problem of complex networks of inconsistent P2P contractual provisions. Still another person advocated that P2P compliance standards ought to follow the model provided by financial accounting, in which a common framework of rules supports transparency and accountability among firms: "What would be helpful, coming out of the P2P [trend], is a 'regulatory compliance balance sheet'—something that is not just a measurement of the compliance program but also of its results. [What's needed is] a common way for outsiders to establish the compliance health of firms." Along a somewhat related line, several participants in the symposium discussed ways in which the government might help to guide P2P in a constructive direction. Although some expressed general skepticism about the role of the government, others observed that the root pressure for P2P originated from key pieces of government policy, most notably the FCPA and federal procurement regulations. At the extreme, it was observed that the government could alternately (1) add to P2P pressure through future legislation, (2) streamline and harmonize the existing pressure by offering standards and recommendations for P2P, or even (3) reduce the pressure, as by making P2P contractual provisions harder to enforce.

A distinct but related strand of discussion in the symposium addressed the role of government resolution agreements as another (potentially) transformative factor in redefining the source of the compliance burden. In context, one salient observation was that recent resolution agreements may have contributed to momentum for P2P compliance by imposing related requirements on settling companies. This is an example of direct government involvement in the P2P field. In a different vein, the question was raised as to whether resolution agreements can or should be viewed as an instrument of broader government policy, moving beyond the specific criminal and civil cases that they resolve. Several symposium participants suggested that the correct answer is no, and that resolutions are neither designed nor intended to have the force of prescriptive authority for companies beyond those that specifically enter into them. Nevertheless, several other participants suggested that purposefully or not, resolution agreements are "sending a message to the marketplace" in how enforcement agencies are approaching the problem of deficient compliance in the context of material misconduct. For better or worse, that signal is likely to be closely examined by firms, and it has the potential to influence compliance behavior and standards more broadly, even when that is not the intent of the regulator. In this light, one symposium participant summed up on the impact of government resolution agreements in this way: "The biggest thing the government can do [to help the compliance field] is simply to be consistent."

Organizational Culture Will Become Even More Important as a C&E Focal Point

A recurring theme in the symposium discussion involved the transformational importance of organizational culture and ethics, as a basic part of the responsibility of the compliance function and of the CECO. Several participants noted that the domain of compliance is broader than the rote enforcement of legal rules because, as one participant succinctly put it: "Compliance without ethics doesn't work. Period." Another person alluded to the Federal Sentencing Guidelines, and its 2004 provision that defines an effective compliance program as one promoting an organizational culture that "encourages ethical behavior," as well as compliance with law. Other participants observed that a similar focus on culture has more recently been emphasized in several resolution agreements and other sources of policy guidance and authority. The focus on culture reflects a fundamental shift in what the compliance function does and in the professional identity of the compliance field. Related discussions touched on a range of perspectives and viewpoints about what compliance programs will look like in the future. One person stressed that the ethical aspect of the compliance function is a defining feature of the profession, and a reflection of the fact that CECOs have a broader social responsibility that exists in tension with their duty of loyalty to their own firms. In a complementary vein, another person observed that the focus on organizational culture, and on the "softer" antecedents to misbehavior within firms, involves a somewhat different skill set from that typically demanded by the GC's office: hence another argument for distinguishing the compliance function from the legal, and for buttressing the unique professional identity of compliance officers. Still another person commented that the ethical norms and values embedded in a firm's culture are important in shaping that firm's compliance risk, and consequently are a focus for risk management and risk mitigation efforts. For all of these reasons, it was suggested that the emphasis on organizational culture is only likely to become more important to compliance programs and CECOs in the future.

On a somewhat related note, several symposium participants also emphasized the "tone at the top" as a prerequisite for ethical organizational culture, and for helping the compliance function achieve what it is supposed to achieve. One person observed: "When [a message of] integrity is coming from the CEO and it's strongly communicated, then [that message] filters through the entire organization. And the role of the board is to make sure that the top guy is talking [this way to] the company." He concluded that absent this kind of executive leadership, compliance programs can too easily become hollow and ineffective exercises. Another person observed that, at the board level, several things need to happen in order for the right tone at the top to be set. In part, boards need to be engaged in structural activities touching on compliance, which include a reporting relationship between the CECO and the board, corresponding risk-assessment practices, and (possibly) a designated board committee with responsibility for compliance. The same symposium participant went on to point out, however, that the board has a deeper responsibility on ethical culture as well: "The company needs to have [and to articulate] its value proposition, with [a culture of] integrity being a major [part]. That value proposition then needs to be tracked with [appropriate] performance measures. The board is responsible for watching to see that this happens." Still another person noted that RAND had addressed the relationship between compliance in the C-suite, and organizational culture, during a previous symposium session in 2013. The takeaway observation was that C-suite values and behaviors can have a profound impact on risk throughout a company, and therefore that the compliance function arguably ought to have influence and some responsibility for C-suite–level engagement. This was identified as another potentially transformational vector for the compliance profession—something that may contribute to pressure for empowering the CECO role and for elevating its prominence within the hierarchy of management.

Boards and Senior Executives Depend on an Independent Compliance Function in Order to Carry Out Their Own Respective Responsibilities

One of the recurring strands of discussion involved the responsibility of boards and executives for compliance, and the potential impact of the evolving compliance field on those two groups. In part, it was observed that the role of boards in compliance oversight depends on having an independent reporting line from the CECO, or else the boards will lack the information to function effectively. This point was raised in the debate over the contours of attorney-client privilege, and how those contours might shape the compliance function going forward. Several participants suggested that whichever way the *Barko* case was resolved,[5] the results could have a dramatic impact on the empowerment of compliance officers—either by reaffirming them as independent voices and resources for their boards or by substantially weakening them. In this light, one person observed: "If privilege overtakes compliance, then you [will] have transformed [the] compliance [function] into nothing more than an arm of the GC." Another person said: "CECOs have the responsibility to speak truth to power, and they must be protected [and strengthened] when doing that." Although the symposium participants expressed diverse views about the ideal management structure for embedding both the CECO and the GC, several argued that the CECO is dedicated to a fundamentally different mission and viewpoint from the GC. More to the point, the empowered CECO role was described as unique because of its emphasis on ethical commitment, broader social welfare considerations, and "cur[ing] the spiral of groupthink within management." In sum, it was suggested that these qualities are central to the value that CECOs offer to their companies, to their boards, and to top management. It was also suggested that these are qualities that could easily be lost if the compliance field is broadly subordinated to, or absorbed by, the legal function within corporations.

---

[5] See *Barko v Halliburton*, No. 1:05-cv-1276 (DDC Mar. 6, 2014). Again, note that following the date of the RAND symposium, the U.S. Court of Appeals for the D.C. Circuit overturned the judgment of the lower court, and ruled that Halliburton's internal investigation fell within the scope of attorney-client privilege. See *In re: Kellogg, Brown & Root*, 2014 WL 2895939 (CADC June 27, 2014).

Complementary themes were also raised in the symposium discussion, touching on the professionalization of compliance as a field. Here again several of the participants talked about the uniqueness of compliance officers and distinct from legal counsel, with the former being defined (in part) by an ethical commitment distinctly broader than a legal advocate's peculiar and single-minded allegiance to the client's expressed wishes. It was noted that as long as lawyers focus on the question of whether they can legally do something, someone else must be present to ask whether they should, or else "lawful but awful" decisions may result. Various points were raised regarding the training of compliance officers, the professional codification of their ethics standards, and how the trend toward professionalization in compliance might develop in the future. Perhaps most salient was the suggestion that the trend directly addresses one of the major concerns now facing top executives and boards. Several symposium participants observed that boards and C-suites have become increasingly concerned with corporate reputational risk in recent years. Again it was suggested that some of the emerging professional attributes of the compliance field, including the underlying commitment to the public good and the obligation to speak truth to power within the management hierarchy, seem well attuned to addressing some aspects of reputational risk—in the form of violations of law, opportunistic and dishonest behavior, and rigidly short-term constructions of self-interest more generally. Put another way, the emerging professional identity of the compliance field may be congruent with directors and top management placing an increasing emphasis on protecting corporate reputation. By empowering the compliance function, management in particular can "tie themselves to the mast," making it harder to succumb to the siren song of profitable misconduct. One symposium participant notably summed up by suggesting that these trends could well be mutually reinforcing in the future.

Effective Compliance Reflects a Balance Between Transparency and Confidentiality

One of the pivotal themes in the symposium discussion involved the balance between confidentiality and transparency as basic facets of the compliance function within any company. This discussion started with the *Barko* case, and with the legal scope of attorney-client privilege, but rapidly expanded to address how transparency forms a basic building block for an effective compliance program. In this vein, several symposium participants observed that undertaking confidential investigations of possible wrongdoing is only one part of the CECO role. Equally important is creating an environment in which employees recognize honesty and fair dealing as corporate basic values, understand formal compliance processes within the company, and see those processes as being carried out in a clear and consistent way. One person commented: "A lot of [what compliance officers do] is nonprivileged for a reason. If the CECO can't tell people [inside the company] about what compliance is doing, or how things are going, then the credibility of the CECO [within the company] will suffer." In particular, it was noted that an excessive emphasis on confidentiality could prevent employees from seeing that the company takes allegations of misconduct seriously, investigates carefully, and imposes consequences when appropriate. Another person suggested that transparency in compliance translates back into corporate culture. It contributes to building engagement among employees, and to the recognition that compliance goes beyond a check-the-box activity, and instead reflects a shared commitment to high standards of workplace integrity and behavior. Still another symposium participant approached these issues somewhat differently, by noting that there would always be situations in which companies need to involve their GCs to conduct privileged and confidential investigations in order to protect against liability risk. The compliance function needs to be cognizant, and an active partner with the GC, in these situations. But the demand for confidentiality nevertheless has to be balanced against the need for transparency, in order for corporate insiders and outsiders to buy into the legitimacy of the compliance function. Another participant said that, as a practical matter, "if everything is privileged (i.e., confidential), nothing is privileged," and that attempting to cast the cloak of attorney-client privilege too broadly risks undermining the claim of privilege in those situations where it is most needed. Without reaching a detailed conclusion on what the correct balance between transparency and confidentiality is, there was consensus among the symposium participants that the evolution of this balance will have a dramatic effect on what compliance programs look like in the future.

Transformational Trends in Compliance Are Likely to Affect and Blend with Each Other

Regarding the future trajectory of the compliance field, one recurring observation in the symposium was simply that there is more than one thing going on in the developing field at once. While the symposium participants were broadly in agreement that vectors such as the P2P trend and the professionalization of compliance as a discipline will be important in the future, there was also an acknowledgment that these trends are bleeding into each other in significant ways. Thus, for example, participants observed that several recent government resolution agreements have included P2P provisions, thereby linking the proliferation of private compliance obligations with the influence of government enforcement efforts. More, the P2P trend was also observed to be bleeding into the professionalization of the field, inasmuch as P2P demands have put pressure on the CECO's independence from business functions that he or she is otherwise responsible for monitoring. Other participants commented on the connection between the professionalization of compliance and CECOs, and the debate over evidentiary privilege and the independence of the compliance function from legal. In context, it was observed that the transformational impact of these various change vectors is complex and likely to be mutually recursive. Put in other words, the compliance field is shifting simultaneously and interactively in the sources of the compliance burden; in the impact and reach of government enforcement efforts; and in the roles, professional identity, ethical obligations, and executive empowerment of compliance practitioners. To the extent that any individual element within this tableau changes (or is radically transformed), other elements are likely to shift in response. Any new paradigm for compliance practice in the future is likely to arise from the blending of multiple trends that are now under way. By extension, the future trajectory of the P2P trend or of the recent legal debates over privilege could wind up reshaping the compliance field much more broadly, and in ways that are difficult to fully foresee.

The Empowered CECO Will Be a Foundational Ingredient in the Transformation of Compliance

One of the basic strands of discussion in the symposium session involved the importance of the empowered CECO, in defining the current state of the art in compliance practice and also as a platform for future development of the field. Several symposium participants offered comments along these lines. One observed: "A rising compliance officer lifts all boats." Another said: "The more stature to the CECO, the better." A third stated that "compliance officers need empowerment" to carry out their role. A fourth person perceived that the attributes of an effective CECO have been written about extensively and include independence, adequate seniority, appropriate resourcing, and a clear performance mandate from top management. Although the symposium participants expressed varied opinions concerning the ideal relationship between the CECO and the GC, there was general agreement that the seniority and empowerment of the CECO ought to match the operating responsibilities that the CECO is expected to perform. Thus, one person pointed out that if "the board depends on the CECO for [a special kind of] information, then [it follows that] the CECO needs to have access and a reporting line to the board." Another participant suggested that if the CECO is expected to broadly influence organizational culture, or to monitor and mitigate C-suite–level risk, then the CECO needs to be appropriately positioned and resourced to be able to do those things. In context, the symposium discussion touched on two additional, related points. The first was historical—namely, that the past decade of evolving policy and practice has helped to elevate the CECO role, congruently with rising expectations for stronger compliance programs and risk management within companies. The second point was forward looking—namely, that several of the transformational vectors now acting on the compliance field seem likely to contribute pressure, moving toward further empowerment and elevation of the CECO role.

4. How Can Boards, Management, Compliance Officers, and Government Respond in Support of More-Effective Compliance?

The final session of the symposium directly addressed several stakeholder groups that are likely to be directly affected by compliance transformation in the future—e.g., boards, C-suite executives, government policymakers, and compliance officers themselves. Symposium participants were asked what kinds of actions each of these stakeholder groups might take, either to try to move the compliance field in a positive direction or to respond to foreseeably changing conditions in compliance in a positive way. Some of the discussion focused on tangible things that CECOs, managers, and others could do differently on the ground in order to contribute to compliance transformation or to a better standard of compliance practice in the near future. Other points in the discussion focused on more normative considerations regarding the ideal structure and aim of compliance in the future and the steps that various stakeholder groups might pursue in order to support those normative visions. Ultimately, the discussion circled back to two basic points. The first was the observation that transformational change in the compliance field is already well under way, partly in connection with the specific vectors discussed in the symposium white papers (e.g., the P2P trend, professionalization, and the debate over privilege). In one sense, then, the question for stakeholders is not whether the compliance field is likely to shift to a new paradigm in the future, but rather how can that shift be influenced in a maximally productive and useful direction? Second, the symposium discussion returned to the idea that boards and senior executives have become increasingly concerned with managing reputation risk for their companies, and that the evolution of compliance is occurring within a broader landscape of corporate governance and responsibility that is also shifting. For boards and executives in particular, the transformation of compliance invites some reflection on the nature of corporate reputation risk and the potential for compliance programs and CECOs to serve as a useful asset in assessing and responding to that risk.

The discussion in this session touched on several other major focal points:

- Boards can take steps to strengthen C&E capability and monitoring efforts.
- Management can focus on both structure and culture in the organization.
- Government can help by setting consistent standards and leading by example.
- Compliance officers can strengthen the field through improved efforts on role definition, professional development, education, and communication.

Boards Can Take Steps to Strengthen C&E Capability and Monitoring Efforts

One of the leading questions posed in the symposium session was: What more should boards be doing on compliance? Several of the responses focused on specific ways that boards can be strengthened in their compliance knowledge and capability. Among the suggestions were adding new directors with professional backgrounds in compliance; strengthening C&E training at the board level; setting up new compliance board committees, or else delegating compliance responsibility to existing board committees (e.g., audit); and increasing the amount of board meeting time that is explicitly devoted to C&E topics. Although multiple participants offered suggestions along these lines, a few others expressed reservations about imposing new (compliance-related) structural requirements and time demands on boards, in light of the reality that many boards are already overloaded with commitments and regulatory, fiduciary, and best-practice "check the box" obligations. In context, one participant noted that the *Caremark* case actually imposed a fairly low bar for boards in terms of their basic legal obligation to focus on compliance issues as an element of fiduciary duty.[6] That participant then raised the question of how far boards should go to strengthen their compliance competency and oversight, and to what end. Others answered that from a board perspective, the appropriate aim for compliance ought to include both preventing violations of law with adverse consequences to shareholders (consistent with *Caremark*) and promoting an ethical organizational culture (consistent with the Federal Sentencing Guidelines). Ultimately, most of the symposium participants agreed that many possible steps for strengthening board awareness and sophistication on C&E issues are straightforward, given the assumption that strengthening boards in this way is a desirable end to pursue.

Several symposium participants offered complementary suggestions regarding steps that boards can take on C&E. One of the suggested steps was contributing to structural reforms within companies, as by building clear C&E performance criteria and incentives into management compensation packages. Other suggestions focused on the softer (cultural) aspects of C&E and the board's role in contributing to it. One person noted that boards are largely responsible for setting the tone at the top, so boards need to lead by example in establishing a culture of integrity, as well as by selecting for integrity at the C-suite level and ensuring that the CEO places a visible priority on integrity through his or her leadership. In a similar vein, another symposium participant suggested that with help from the CECO, the board ought actively to monitor ethical organizational ethical culture over time, such as via employee and management surveys. In turn, the conversation pivoted back to the relationship between the CECO and the board, and the importance to the board of ensuring a strong relationship and independent reporting channel with the CECO. One participant put it this way: "What worries me [at the

[6] *In re Caremark International Inc. Derivative Litigation*, 698 A.2d 959 (Del. Ch. 1996).

board level] is the tendency to emphasize form over substance [in dealing with compliance]." Along the same line, others suggested that CECO reporting to the board ought to be substantive rather than perfunctory, that the board ought to spend meaningful time with the CECO in assessing the most important C&E challenges facing the company, and that, ultimately, compliance risk ties back to reputation risk, which is often a high-priority topic for boards.

Management Can Focus on Both Structure and Culture in the Organization

Another strand of the discussion focused on the things that senior management and the C-suite can do to improve compliance performance and to reduce risk within the organization—here again broadly in the service of *transforming* compliance. Some of the suggestions went back to the tone at the top, and to the CEO and other senior executives communicating the importance of integrity and ethical culture in the workplace while modeling their commitment through their own behavior. Other suggestions for the C-suite included institutionalizing the measurement of corporate culture, monitoring related performance metrics in the same manner that financial performance metrics are monitored, providing clear standards and expectations for C&E performance among line managers, establishing corresponding assessment- and performance-based rewards for managers, and more formally drawing on ethical leadership criteria when making hiring and promotion decisions. One symposium participant underlined the importance of incentive structures for desired compliance activity, such that people within the company get rewarded for behaviors that management wants to cultivate, and no one is exempt from consequences for ethical deviance. Another participant emphasized a different point in arguing that line management ideally needs to take responsibility for ensuring appropriate compliance performance throughout the organization. In context, it was observed that the role of the CECO includes putting the right compliance standards and processes in place, but that ultimate responsibility for compliance still has to be broadly owned by managers and employees outside the compliance function. In turn, it was suggested that this kind of ownership ties back to expectations and incentives laid down by senior management. Finally, empowerment of the CECO was raised as another obvious step that senior management can undertake to improve compliance performance. Apart from elevating the compliance function and communicating its importance, it was suggested that empowering the CECO can also help the C-suite in fulfilling its own C&E oversight responsibility, such as by carrying out appropriate risk-assessment activities across the entire firm.

Government Can Help by Setting Consistent Standards and Leading by Example

A major point of discussion involved the role of government and things that government could do in the service of better compliance performance in organizations. Symposium participants expressed some differences of opinion over how active government should ideally be in seeking to harmonize standards for P2P compliance, or in using resolution agreements to try to drive corporate compliance activity more broadly. Notably, some participants thought that more government involvement along these lines might be a good step to take, while others expressed skepticism. With this being said, there was a series of other suggestions for pragmatic steps that government might take to strengthen compliance programs in the future. One person repeated that "the biggest thing that government can do to help is to be consistent"—namely, by developing compliance standards and enforcement policies that apply in a transparent, coherent, and uniform way. Another person said that "one of the best things that government can do is to lead by example," such as by setting up strong compliance programs in government agencies, and thereby modeling the same practices and behavior that private sector companies are expected to exhibit. Still another person suggested that government ought to "look for opportunities to visibly recognize the value of compliance programs," so that the stick of enforcement is more often seen to be tempered by the carrot of leniency for strong programs. One of the recurring themes in the discussion was the empowerment of CECOs and the ways in which government actors might build on related policies already codified in the Federal Sentencing Guidelines and other places. One tactical suggestion along this line involved enforcement agencies *not* targeting CECOs for prosecution for the misconduct of others, absent evidence of direct misconduct or active condonation by them. It was observed that by making the CECO a focal point for certifications of substantive compliance, prosecution and individual liability might plausibly have a chilling effect on CECOs generally, and on the compliance programs they lead. A somewhat related suggestion was the government making stronger efforts to protect CECOs from workplace retaliation, and from the perverse effects of retaliation, when responding to incidents of material fraud and misbehavior involving senior management within a company.

Compliance Officers Can Strengthen the Field Through Improved Efforts on Role Definition, Professional Development, Education, and Communication

One of the ultimate strands of discussion during the symposium session involved steps that compliance officers can take in order to strengthen the field and compliance practice in the future. Building on the professionalism white paper authored by Joseph Murphy, several symposium participants talked about the value of broadly adopting or extending a formal code of ethics and "model rules of conduct" for compliance practitioners. It was suggested that such rules can serve as an important element in helping to professionalize the field, and also in supporting the CECO to take difficult stands (when necessary) within the company. As one person observed along related lines: "Somebody has to have the guts at some point to say 'no'—that's an important part of the compliance job." Others suggested a range of possible action items for compliance practitioners, including a reaffirmation of, and spotlight on, the ethical aspects of the CECO role; development of a new educational curriculum and materials for business schools and law schools to encourage high-quality new entrants into the profession; and more-targeted outreach to journalists and others outside the compliance community, both to provide education about the actual role of compliance officers and to help shape outside expectations of the field. It was suggested that these are all steps available to compliance practitioners that could help make the compliance field stronger. Beyond these sorts of recommendations, two other related points were made in discussion. The first involved the basic definition of what it is that compliance officers do, and what role they play within their organizations. Beyond helping to define their own roles, it was suggested that compliance officers also need to communicate a key message within their companies: The existence of a compliance program does not exculpate the rest of the organization from taking direct responsibility for compliance performance and shortcomings. Second, and in a different vein, it was observed that the CECO role can involve a difficult balance between occasionally setting limits (i.e., saying no) to senior management and finding ways to work collaboratively and constructively with senior management on a day-to-day basis. Both aspects of the CECO role were underlined as being important to success, and it was suggested understanding the duality might move compliance practitioners a step closer to better carrying out both sides of the role.

Appendix A. Symposium Agenda

RAND Center for Corporate Ethics and Governance

Transforming Compliance:
Emerging Paradigms for Boards, Management, Compliance Officers, and Government

May 28, 2014
RAND Corporation, Pentagon City
1200 South Hayes Street, Arlington, VA 22202

Sponsored by

NYSE GOVERNANCE SERVICES

Symposium Chair: Dr. Michael D. Greenberg
Symposium Co-Chair: Donna C. Boehme

Agenda

1:00 p.m. **Welcome and Introductory Remarks**
Michael D. Greenberg, Director, RAND Center for Corporate Ethics & Governance
Donna C. Boehme, Principal, Compliance Strategists, LLC

1:15 p.m. **Invited Remarks from White Paper Authors**
Introductions by Donna C. Boehme, Principal, Compliance Strategists LLC

- The Privatization of Compliance
  Scott Killingsworth, Partner, Bryan Cave
- Compliance and Ethics as a Profession – In the Public Interest
  Joseph Murphy, Director of Public Policy, Society for Corporate Compliance and Ethics
- Redefining the Relationship of the General Counsel and Chief Compliance Officer
  Michael Volkov, CEO and Owner, The Volkov Law Group LLC
- Learning the Hard Way: Ethics and Compliance Lessons Gleaned from Recent United States Settlement Agreements
  Peter Jaffe, Chief Ethics and Compliance Officer, AES Corporation
  Michael Diamant, Partner, Gibson Dunn

2:15 p.m. **Roundtable Session 1**: What is the emerging paradigm for compliance programs of the future, and what are the implications for boards, management, compliance officers and government?

3:45 p.m. Break

4:00 p.m. **Roundtable Session 2:** How could each of the above constituency groups respond, in support of more effective compliance? What are the top priority action items for each group?

5:30 p.m. **Closing Remarks**
Michael D. Greenberg, RAND Corporation

6:00 p.m. **Reception and Dinner**
Ritz Carlton, Pentagon City
Featured Speaker: Kathleen Grilli, General Counsel, U.S. Sentencing Commission
"Days of Future Past: Why the Path to the Next Generation of Compliance and Ethics Programs Has Already been Paved"

Appendix B. Symposium Participants

TRANSFORMING COMPLIANCE: AN EMERGING PARADIGM FOR BOARDS, MANAGEMENT, COMPLIANCE OFFICERS AND GOVERNMENT

Roundtable Conference
RAND Center for Corporate Ethics & Governance
MAY 28, 2014

SYMPOSIUM PARTICIPANT LIST

Michael Greenberg (Symposium Chair)
Director, RAND Center for Corp. Ethics and Governance

Donna C. Boehme (Symposium Co-Chair)
Principal, Compliance Strategists LLC

Michael S. Diamant
Partner, Gibson, Dunn & Crutcher

Peter E. Jaffe
Chief Ethics and Compliance Officer, AES Corporation

Scott Killingsworth
Partner, Bryan Cave LLP

Joseph E. Murphy
Senior Advisor, Compliance Strategists LLC

Michael Volkov
CEO and Owner, The Volkov Law Group LLC

Karen Bertha
Chief Ethics & Compliance Officer, MCR, LLC

Erica Salmon Byrne
Executive Vice President, Compliance & Governance Solutions

Stephen Cohen
Associate Director, Enforcement Division, U.S. Securities & Exchange Commission

Keith T. Darcy
Executive Director (Ret), Ethics & Compliance Officer Assn, Senior Advisor, Deloitte

John DeLong
Director of Compliance, National Security Agency

Paula Desio
Former Deputy General Counsel, USSC; Principal, Professional Ethics Consulting LLC

Charles Elson
Edgar S. Woolard, Jr. Chair in Corporate Governance and the Director of the John L. Weinberg Center for Corporate Governance at the University of Delaware

Harold Fogelberg
Director, Center for Business Ethics, Belmont University

Patrick J. Gnazzo
Former SVP and General Manager, U.S. Public Sector, CA, Inc.; Principal, Better Business Practices LLC

Ellen Hunt
Director, Ethics & Compliance, Office of General Counsel, AARP

Jack B. Jacobs
Justice, Supreme Court of Delaware

Stephen Kohn
Executive Director, National Whistleblower Center

Ann McLaughlin Korologos
Former U.S. Secretary of Labor

Bradley Lucido
SVP and Chief Compliance Officer, and Deputy General Counsel, Mass Mutual Financial Group

Cindy Moehring
SVP and Global Chief Ethics Officer, WalMart Stores Inc.

Judith L. Nocito
Senior Advisor, Compliance Strategists LLC; Former Director of Global Compliance, Alcoa Inc.

Edward A. Ryan
Executive Vice President and General Counsel, Marriott International, Inc

Michael Scher
Contributing Editor, FCPA Blog

Alan Yuspeh
Senior Vice President and Chief Ethics and Compliance Officer, Hospital Corporation of America (HCA Holdings, Inc)

Appendix C. Invited Papers from Symposium Participants

The Privatization of Compliance

Scott Killingsworth, Partner
Bryan Cave LLP

"As appropriate, a large organization should encourage small organizations (especially those that have, or seek to have, a business relationship with the large organization) to implement effective compliance and ethics programs."
U.S. Sentencing Commission[1]

Introduction

Achieving consistent legal compliance in today's regulatory environment is a challenge severe enough to keep compliance officers awake at night and one at which even well-managed companies regularly fail. But besides coping with governmental oversight and legal enforcement, companies now face a growing array of both substantive and process-oriented compliance obligations imposed by trading partners and other private organizations, sometimes but not always instigated by the government. Embodied in contract clauses and codes of conduct for business partners, these obligations often go beyond mere compliance with law and address the methods by which compliance is assured. They create new compliance obligations and enforcement mechanisms and touch upon the structure, design, priorities, functions and administration of corporate ethics and compliance programs. And these obligations are contagious: increasingly accountable not only for their own compliance but also that of their supply chains, companies must seek corresponding contractual assurances upstream. Compliance is becoming privatized, and privatization is going viral.

A Qualitative Shift

There has been an element of privatization in the compliance arena at least since the Federal Sentencing Guidelines for Organizations[2] were established. After all, the point of the Sentencing Guidelines is to leverage the government's limited regulatory and enforcement resources by offering a strong incentive for companies to take on more of the state's prevention, detection and

---

[1] U.S. Sentencing Commission, Guidelines Manual, §8B2 (November, 2013), commentary quoted is at p. 499 and was added effective November 2004 by Amendment 673. Available online at http://www.ussc.gov/guidelines-manual/2013/2013-8b21 (visited June 6, 2014).

[2] An Overview of the Federal Sentencing Guidelines, http://www.ussc.gov/sites/default/files/pdf/about/overview/Overview_Federal_Sentencing_Guidelines.pdf (visited June 6, 2014).

enforcement burden. Corporate compliance programs augment state oversight by performing tasks that governments lack the resources or the line-of-sight to do efficiently.

But that state-incentivized privatization model still reflects the traditional vertical, two-party relationship between government and the governed. The new wave of privatization is horizontal, networked, and qualitatively different. The Sentencing Guidelines model simply mitigates the risk of compliance failure. It does not expose companies to new forms of risk, liabilities or forfeitures or to the possibility of multiple conflicting standards, but private-to-private (P2P) compliance may do so. Program elements and ethical policies become contractual obligations, vulnerable to such contractual remedies as indemnities, damages, audits, default declarations, loan acceleration and termination. P2P compliance is reshaping the compliance task portfolio and raising new questions about who is answerable to whom, both internally and across company boundaries.

Private compliance pressures may originate from any point in the value chain: suppliers, customers, capital markets, insurers. Compliance officers may find themselves caught in the middle between demanding customers and reluctant suppliers, or, in the other direction, between manufacturers vitally interested in how their products reach market and resellers seeking the shortest route to revenue.[3] They may be simultaneously pitted against their own colleagues in charge of operations, procurement, business acquisition and contracting. And unlike the Sentencing Guidelines and most other government leniency programs, many of the privatized compliance requirements are truly mandatory—at least if you want to do business with the other party.

A Positive Direction

From Apple[4] to Zoetis,[5] major corporations are requiring their business associates to commit to third-party codes of conduct (P2P Codes) and related contract clauses. This trend signals a growing appreciation that enterprises across the value chain share one another's reputational and compliance risks, and that compliance processes play an important role in translating legal commands into lawful conduct. It reflects an awareness that if you are dependent on a business partner to keep you out of legal trouble, it might pay to take an interest in how they intend to accomplish that.

By recasting compliance and ethics from a vertical, state-imposed constraint on business to an integral, horizontal expectation of how business is done, P2P compliance encourages the

---

[3] For example, customers may exert pressures regarding the sourcing of raw materials from regions that are known for forced labor or are involved in conflict, or regarding the social or environmental impacts of extractive activities; while manufacturers and value-added sellers may have a strong interest in pushing anti-corruption compliance through their sales and distribution channel.

[4] The Apple Supplier Code of Conduct is available at https://www.apple.com/supplier-responsibility/pdf/Apple_Supplier_Code_of_Conduct.pdf (visited June 6, 2014).

[5] The Zoetis Supplier Conduct Principles and an accompanying Position Statement are available at http://www.zoetis.com/supplier-information (visited June 6, 2014).

adoption of best practices both as a cultural norm and, critically, as a path to profit. Coming now from external business partners rather than just the internal ethics and compliance staff, this message has the potential to re-orient some attitudes and remove some ethical blinders. As more businesses are forced by their counterparties to examine their compliance processes and routinely accept business and legal consequences for them, we can expect increases in overall investment in compliance, in the scope and robustness of the average compliance program, and in ambient awareness of compliance issues outside the compliance, audit, and legal staffs. The viral nature of the process, in which each participant can exert pressure on a large number of direct and indirect upstream or downstream parties, while simultaneously fielding demands from other members of its value chain, suggests that the trend will continue and its influence will grow.

Historically, most P2P Codes have covered key integrity risks and issues of corporate social responsibility at the level of policy rather than of procedure—and at this level they have reflected broad consensus on compliance best practices and accepted principles of corporate responsibility. They have been easy to accept without fear of adverse side effects, and most still are. But the newer trends of adding process or "how-to" components, of more granular and prescriptive drafting, and of embedding P2P Codes more firmly in a contractual mesh raise a note of caution. We can hope that as P2P assurances become more routine, a consensus will emerge around generally accepted practices for demanding and enforcing assurances from one's counterparty and its value chain. Today, however, P2P compliance is in its awkward, adolescent phase. Before turning to some of the challenges, let's review how we got here and where we are.

Origins and Protagonists

We can trace the origins of this trend to three main protagonists: governments, both in their sovereign roles and as customers; the human rights/corporate social responsibility movement; and companies themselves.

Government Instigation in the Enforcement and Procurement Spheres

Blockbuster fines, civil penalties and disgorgements, monitorships and burdensome settlement agreements are attention-getters. They provide not only object lessons about compliance risk—and lately, third-party risk especially—but also a "bully pulpit" from which officials can provide specific guidance to an increasingly attentive audience about compliance program features that will affect enforcement decisions. For example, FCPA deferred/non-prosecution agreements[6] today send a message by routinely requiring settling defendants to institute appropriate compliance process controls over business associates,[7] such as advance due diligence and

---

[6] *See*, e.g., Ralph Lauren Non-Prosecution Agreement, April 22, 2013, Attachment B, pp. B-2 through B-7, available at http://www.justice.gov/criminal/fraud/fcpa/cases/ralph-lauren/Ralph-Lauren.-NPA-Executed.pdf (visited June 6, 2014).

[7] The required third-party controls apply, "where necessary and appropriate," to a very broad class: "outside parties acting on behalf of the Company in a foreign jurisdiction, including but not limited to, agents and intermediaries,

ongoing oversight, "flowing down"[8] codes of conduct, imposing training requirements, and securing contractual commitments covering recordkeeping, audit rights, vendor compliance undertakings, and associated termination rights—all principles that are echoed in more conventional DOJ guidance[9] and in official guidance on the U.K. Bribery Act[10] as well. Similarly, in 2013 the Office of the Comptroller of the Currency offered risk management guidelines to financial institutions for critical services contracts, including requirements for due diligence evaluations of suppliers' legal and regulatory compliance programs, audit rights over their risk management and internal controls, and ongoing monitoring and remediation activities.[11] This kind of "advice" is ignored at one's peril.

The government's role as a customer may be even more influential, at least in the US. All holders of large federal contracts are now required to institute compliance programs that track the Sentencing Guidelines' (otherwise voluntary) criteria, and are specifically required to contractually flow down these obligations to large subcontractors.[12] This general procurement rule is supplemented by a growing number of topic-specific supply-chain diligence provisions in areas as diverse as human trafficking and information security for controlled technical information.[13]

The Human Rights and Corporate Social Responsibility Movement

The role of the human rights and corporate social responsibility movement, including advocacy groups and multinational NGOs, is quite distinct from that of the state, both in origins and in aims. Focused on global human rights, environmental and social issues, and corruption, and on the ambivalent economic interactions between developed and undeveloped nations, NGOs such as the International Labor Organization, the OECD, the World Bank, the United Nations and the International Chamber of Commerce (ICC) have campaigned for global acceptance and

---

consultants, representatives, distributors, teaming partners, contractors and suppliers, consortia, and joint venture partners."

[8] To "flow down" a contractual or code requirement is to impose it upon third parties representing successive links in a contracting chain, such as subcontractors and suppliers, or distributors and sales agents. Ordinarily this is done by requiring each link to incorporate an identical or equivalent clause in its contract with the next link, sometimes ad infinitum.

[9] *See*, e.g., A Resource Guide to the U.S. Foreign Corrupt Practices Act, issued November 20, 2012, available at www.justice.gov/criminal/fraud/fcpa (visited June 6, 2014), and DOJ Opinions 08-02, June 2008 and 10-02, July 2010, available at www.justice.gov/criminal/fraud/fcpa/opinion (June 6, 2014).

[10] Ministry of Justice, The Bribery Act 2010 Guidance, available at http://www.justice.gov.uk/downloads/legislation/bribery-act-2010-guidance.pdf (June 6, 2014).

[11] Office of the Comptroller of the Currency, OCC Bulletin 2013-29, Risk Management Guidance for Third-Party Relationships.

[12] *See* Federal Acquisition Regulation (FAR) §52.203-13. A "large" contract or subcontract is one with a value of at least $5 million and a performance period of at least 120 days, to be performed at least partly within the United States.

[13] *See* (as to human trafficking) Executive Order 13627, "Strengthening Protections Against Trafficking in Persons in Federal Contracts" and FAR §22.1703 et seq., FAR § 52.212-5, and (as to supply chain information security) FAR Subpart 239.703 and §252.239-7017 et seq.

implementation of ethical business standards—in some cases implementing them with integrity standards for their own suppliers.[14] In parallel, advocacy groups such as Friends of the Earth and the Rainforest Action Network have pursued issue-oriented campaigns to change business practices through the court of public opinion, often targeting specific entities or industries.[15] These NGO campaigns and the principles they stand for claim legitimacy from world community consensus rather than from national legislation; and they seek implementation of this collective conscience in the business world via the exertion of influence by one private organization upon another.

An illustrative product of this type of effort is the Equator Principles,[16] a voluntary private compact among 78 major financial institutions that sets environmental and social impact standards for the activities of commercial banks in global project finance. Under these principles, the banks must require project-finance borrowers to implement an "environmental, social, health and safety management system . . . including policies, management programs and plans, procedures, requirements, performance indicators, responsibilities, training and periodic audits and inspections with respect to Environmental or Social Matters"—essentially, a full-blown environmental and social compliance program—backed up by independent consultants who report to the banks. The associated loan agreements include covenants, representations, warranties, and events of default keyed to the program's goals.

The Equator Principles took a number of years to become fully institutionalized and to gain a critical mass of adherents. By contrast, within three months after the recent Rana Plaza factory collapse, major customers of the Bangladesh garment industry established both the Accord on Fire and Building Safety in Bangladesh[17] and the competing Alliance for Bangladesh Worker Safety.[18] Both initiatives mandate independent inspections, remediation, training, worker reporting mechanisms, and required cooperation from the suppliers. Multinationals have gotten the supply-chain compliance message and have learned to respond decisively to failures.

Corporate Developments

Apart from reacting to the direct external pressures just outlined, companies have been forced to come to grips internally with the reputational, legal, and financial risk implications of the global trend towards disaggregation of the enterprise and the consequent atomization of the supply chain across national boundaries. Improved enterprise risk and compliance management has

---

[14] *See* UN Supplier Code of Conduct, September 2013, available at http://www.un.org/depts/ptd/pdf/conduct_english.pdf (visited June 6, 2014).

[15] *See* O'Sullivan, infra note 16, pp 108–112.

[16] Niamh A. O'Sullivan, Social Accountability and the Finance Sector: The Case of Equator Principles (EP) Institutionalisation (doctoral dissertation 2010), available at dare.uva.nl/document/185897 (visited June 6, 2014).

[17] According on Fire and Building Safety in Bangladesh, http://bangladeshaccord.org/wp-content/uploads/2013/10/the_accord.pdf (visited June 6, 2014).

[18] About the Alliance for Bangladesh Worker Safety, http://www.bangladeshworkersafety.org/about/about-the-alliance (visited June 6, 2014).

focused attention on the exponential increase in third-party exposure that companies incurred by outsourcing of all but their "core" functions. Headlines provide daily reminders that outsourcing a critical, compliance-sensitive function does not outsource the associated reputational, legal or financial risk. Companies have responded by re-investing in managing and monitoring business partners' compliance just as they do product quality.[19] As with quality, the management tools employed include direct monitoring and auditing, explicit contractual allocation of compliance responsibilities and risks, and requiring the business associate to institute and flow down specified compliance policies, procedures and processes.

This trend is not just about the product supply chain; it is proliferating in other business relationships as well. An important recent development is the emergence of compliance risk management as a prerequisite for conventional access to capital. Promising to obey the law is no longer enough; today, corporate credit agreements and securities underwriting agreements commonly include additional representations and covenants that the borrower/issuer has "implemented and maintains policies and procedures designed to ensure, and which are reasonably expected to continue to ensure, compliance" with specified laws, including the FCPA and other anticorruption legislation, Office of Foreign Assets Control sanctions, anti-money laundering legislation, the USA PATRIOT Act, securities disclosure requirements and insider trading prohibitions for public companies, and industry-specific regulations such as HIPAA and information security requirements. Credit rating agencies have revealed that they are examining compliance markers for red flags as part of their ratings process,[20] and at least one insurer requires those seeking FCPA investigation-cost insurance to have their compliance programs benchmarked by a third party.[21]

The potential impact of this recent market focus on effective corporate compliance systems reaches well beyond access to capital. In late 2012 a major proxy advisory firm announced that it will recommend voting against retention of directors, in uncontested elections, where there has been a material compliance failure.[22] By May 2014 it had done so.[23]

---

[19] One effect of more engaged management of outsourced functions is that it requires surrendering some of the cost savings that fueled the outsourcing epidemic in the first place. This swing of the pendulum is part of a larger reconsideration of the balance between risks and rewards of outsourcing at a more granular level than in the past. For example, a similar adjustment seems to have occurred in a related quarter as "companies have reversed a trend toward reducing the number of suppliers in order to cut costs and have added them to reduce risk" of supply-chain disruption. See Jaeger, "Are Firms Lacking in Supply Chain Management?" Compliance Week, November 2013, page 43.

[20] *See* Standard & Poor's Ratings Direct Methodology: Management and Governance Credit Factors for Corporate Entities and Insurers, November 13, 2012, Table 2 and items 47, 61 and 62.

[21] Author background interview with a Senior Vice President of a major insurance broker.

[22] *See* ISS U.S. Corporate Governance Policy 2013 Updates, November 16, 2012, citing the 2010 BP Deepwater Horizon spill and News Corporation UK's 2011 integrity scandal as material failures of board risk oversight.

[23] *See* Paul Ziobro and Joann Lublin, "Ouster of Target Directors is Urged," Wall Street Journal, May 29, 2014, p. B2. ISS recommended "no" votes on seven incumbent directors of Target Corporation, claiming that inadequacies in risk oversight had set the stage for the 2013 data breach.

The Anti-Corruption Archetype

Needless to say, these themes of governmental enforcement and procurement mandates, corporate social responsibility, and risk management across the global supply chain all converge upon the problem of official corruption, and anyone curious about the future of privatized compliance should consider the current state of anti-corruption compliance. Enforcement of anti-corruption laws has reached new heights and, encouraged by the OECD anti-bribery convention,[24] national anticorruption laws continue to proliferate. Several prominent NGOs, including the World Economic Forum,[25] Transparency International,[26] the ICC,[27] the World Bank,[28] and the OECD itself[29] have published detailed guidance on third-party compliance management, guidance that universally includes due diligence, flow-down of anti-corruption policies, training and communication, documentation of business associates' compliance efforts, and imposition of audit rights, ongoing monitoring, and contract remedies such as termination.[30] The debates about best practices are settled, save for skirmishes over when they can be practically applied.

These recommendations have been implemented by a growing number of companies, albeit on a risk-prioritized basis.[31] Third-party due diligence is commonplace and anti-bribery provisions appear frequently in international contracts and universally in P2P Codes, quite often with domino-style flow-down requirements. With this pattern firmly established, code and contract language that was originally drafted only for the anti-corruption context is now being extended to cover other high-priority compliance domains such as export sanctions, money laundering, data privacy and conflict minerals. With this growing adaptation of accepted anti-corruption methodology to other risks,[32] "FCPA" could stand for Future Compliance Paradigm Adopted.

---

[24] OECD, Convention on Combating Bribery of Public Officials in International Business Transactions, available at http://www.oecd.org/daf/anti-bribery/oecdantibriberyconvention.htm (visited June 9, 2014).

[25] World Economic Forum, Partnering against Corruption—Principles for Countering Bribery, 2009.

[26] Transparency International, Business Principles for Countering Bribery, 2013.

[27] International Chamber of Commerce, ICC Rules on Combating Corruption, 2011.

[28] World Bank Integrity Compliance Guidelines, 2010. The principal function of these guidelines is to establish preconditions for ending a noncompliant supplier's debarment from participating in World Bank-financed projects.

[29] OECD Guidelines for Multinational Enterprises, 2011, available at http://www.oecd.org/daf/inv/mne/oecdguidelinesformultinationalenterprises.htm (visited June 9, 2014).

[30] The ICC even offers a booklet of suggested contract clauses, ICC Anti-corruption Clause, ICC Publication No. 740E, 2012.

[31] *See* Dow Jones Anti-Corruption Survey Results 2014 showing inter alia that 82% of survey respondents maintained anticorruption programs, 77% perform due diligence on new partners, 53% rank partners by risk and 35% train their business partners.

[32] *See*, e.g., OCC Bulletin 2013-29, supra note 11, which addresses not only a variety of compliance risks but also strategic, operational, reputational and credit risk.

Codes, Contracts, and Consequences

As mentioned, third-party compliance obligations are increasingly imposed contractually—either within a commercial contract, through a separate P2P Code, or, commonly, together by incorporation of the P2P Code into the contract. As an alternative, business associates are sometimes asked to ensure compliance with the other party's internal code of conduct, which may include provisions specific to third parties.[33] Even where there is no formal contract, a company may impose due diligence, P2P Codes, monitoring and auditing as a precondition for beginning or continuing a business relationship.

P2P Codes commonly contain several distinct types of provisions: broad human rights, labor and corporate social responsibility standards; ethical rules governing relationship issues such as conflicts of interest and gifts and entertainment; requirements to obey specific laws of concern and laws generally; and procedural rules such as the right to audit the partner's records or train its personnel. Process and structural rules may be imposed on the partner's compliance activities, such as requirements to establish management accountability; develop appropriate policies and procedures; maintain an anonymous reporting system and an anti-retaliation policy; train employees; conduct periodic audits, risk assessments and remediation; and of course, sometimes to cascade these program elements to downstream associates.[34]

Many P2P Codes also include provisions of a more traditionally "contractual" nature, such as terms governing intellectual property, use of assets, subcontracting, information security, business continuity, media relations, and statements imposing strict and apparently unlimited liability for subcontractor compliance. Meanwhile, the related business contract will likely contain its own representations, warranties and covenants imposing compliance obligations, often of a detailed and context-sensitive kind.

Needless to say, neither P2P Codes nor contractual compliance terms are uniform across contracting parties, and even a single party's P2P Code and its contractual compliance provisions are often written by different people in different departments, with little or no coordination. Some codes suffer from multiple authorship by specialists with different agendas, adding both

---

[33] See Ronald Berenbeim, "Finding a Delicate Balance: Third-Party Ethics Program Requirements," a Conference Board-Ethics and Compliance Officers' Association Survey (PowerPoint presentation available at http://www.13iacc.org/files/Third_Party_Ethics.pptx), October 31, 2008, finding that at that time 69% of respondents' internal codes purported to apply to third parties, while 25% of respondents had a separate P2P Code. One impetus for adopting P2P Codes is that stretching an internal employee code to cover a wide variety of third-party business partners and relationships can present thorny questions of interpretation and application.

[34] Notably, all of these compliance-program elements are required or recommended in two leading industry model P2P Codes and accompanying guidance: See Electronic Industry Citizenship Coalition® Code of Conduct, available at http://www.eicc.info/documents/EICCCodeofConductEnglish.pdf (visited June 9, 2014), and the Pharmaceutical Industry Principles for Responsible Supply Chain Management and its Implementation Guidance, available respectively at www.pharmaceuticalsupplychain.org/downloads/psci_principles.pdf (visited June 9, 2014), and www.pharmaceuticalsupplychain.org/downloads/psci_guidance.pdf (visited June 9, 2014).

length and a fluctuating level of detail.[35] All this heterogeneity, combined with the wandering boundary between code and contract, can lead to mischief.

The foremost problem is that of remedies: a P2P Code may be expressly incorporated into a contract or may refer to one, with either a clear statement or a fuzzy implication that all contractual remedies apply. When made contractual, even an existing obligation to comply with a law automatically acquires a "private right of action" for damages or other contract remedies, whether the law's regulatory architecture includes one or not. Duties once owed only to specific parties such as employees or consumers are now enforceable by business partners. Likewise, matters of corporate social responsibility or sustainability, once voluntary and ethical, become mandatory and legal. And the standard remedies provided by contract law may be supplemented by custom remedies such as self-help, clawbacks, liquidated damages, suspensions, or debarment.

Given the usual inclusion of precatory, aspirational, and social-responsibility provisions in P2P Codes as well as the common use of debatable terms like "fair," "responsible," "ethical," and "human rights," application of many contractual remedies may simply be inappropriate. It may be reasonable to assume liability for damages, and even to indemnify your business associate, if you get them into regulatory trouble while performing a critical outsourced function—but does it make sense to risk a forfeiture of amounts due, a clawback of amounts paid, or a termination without right to cure if a labor-rights violation is discovered in an unrelated part of your business, or elsewhere in your supply or distribution chain?

The point is that if we are going to turn a compliance code into a contract, we need to consider all the same questions of reasonableness, proportionality and draftsmanship that we ask with any other contract obligations, and in some cases we will need different answers. Experience suggests that this type of legal analysis is the exception rather than the rule. To the contrary, there is anecdotal evidence that, having discovered that P2P Codes are seldom reviewed for contractual liability, some procurement or legal staffs have moved one-sided contract terms into their codes, where the omission of customary contractual exceptions and protections is less likely to trigger negotiation. At a minimum, P2P Codes regularly fail to consider predictable, legitimate interests of the other party that would ordinarily be accommodated in a negotiated contract.[36] This combination of creeping contractualism and

---

[35] The inconsistent tone, level of detail, and peripatetic coverage of some codes seem proof of a maxim usually attributed to H. G. Wells: "No passion in the world is equal to the passion to alter someone else's draft."

[36] A few examples of issues raised by partisan or careless drafting will suffice. Audit provisions in P2P Codes are often unrestricted in scope and lack protections for such concerns as confidentiality, waiver of attorney-client privilege, or competition-law exposure. Sweeping code provisions for surprise inspections and private employee interviews, designed for use in connection with human rights and labor issues in developing countries, take on a different flavor in the complex legal framework of the developed world. Zero-tolerance prohibitions on investment in suppliers by public officials or their families are not unheard of, and some P2P Codes require notification if any of the business partner's employees or their relatives have any financial interest in the code's sponsor—all this in this age of public companies, mutual funds and 401Ks. There is irony in receiving by ordinary e-mail a proposed P2P Code that requires encryption of all information sent over the Internet. And some companies seem to feel that

careless or predatory drafting leads in the wrong direction as compliance risk, immune to the laws of physics, expands via contracting.

The problem of impractical or unfair P2P compliance obligations is only made worse by the fact that vastly unequal bargaining power can pop up at any point in the value chain. Imagine the plight of a specialty distributor caught between the P2P Codes of a major manufacturer and a retailer dominant in the key market segment, each expecting their code provisions to be flowed through to the other. Even powerful market participants may trigger unexpected risks if they use their bargaining leverage too bluntly. If your P2P compliance demands are nonnegotiable and everyone accepts them because they must, how can you distinguish between those who sincerely intend to comply and those who are actually most cynical and least likely to comply? Negotiation, at least, shows that your counterparty takes the matter seriously. And if you have audit or training rights but do not exercise them, or if you do not insist on receiving the required reports or evaluate them when received, do you think you have effectively transferred the risk? Will a prosecutor equate your contractual risk-transfer provisions with a sincere effort to ensure compliance?

The Compliance Officer's Dilemma

If P2P compliance is in its awkward adolescence, so are the processes by which many companies confront it. Not surprisingly, many incoming P2P Codes and compliance provisions are never seen outside the procurement, sales or business development offices where they first land, and as a result companies take on unanticipated, un-bargained-for obligations. As the volume, sophistication, and associated risks of P2P compliance requests continue to grow, they will demand an organized response, led and coordinated by the compliance team.

An appropriate response to the P2P challenge must cope with a number of mismatches evident from the earlier discussion:

- the mismatch between the compliance team's core role of providing objective, independent oversight of compliance risks, and the need to participate actively in the business function of negotiating vital commercial transactions that directly impact the compliance mission;
- the mismatch between the scope of a given P2P Code (including, for example, issues of sustainability, corporate social responsibility, business continuity, information security, etc.) and the core mandate and competencies of the compliance team;
- the mismatch between the goals, priorities, and timelines of the compliance function and those of the sales, business development, and procurement functions where incoming P2P demands are triggered and received;
- the possible mismatch between the compliance activities and priorities demanded by third parties and those of the company;

investment bankers and lawyers should not be allowed to work more than 48 hours a week. Breach of any of these unrealistic requirements could be used as grounds for a pretextual contract termination, or withholding of payment.

- mismatches between P2P compliance demands, such as audit rights, and business objectives such as protecting one's competitively sensitive information or the trade secrets or personal information of third parties;
- and not least, the mismatch between the existing budget and resources of the compliance function and the burgeoning and always-urgent workload all this implies.

P2P compliance demands accentuate the inherent tension between compliance priorities and short-term operational goals, simply because they occur at such critical points in the operational cycle: the initiation of procurement, sales, or financing relationships. On the incoming side, P2P demands could present the compliance officer with a Hobson's choice of either disapproving a transaction or agreeing to unreasonable compliance terms. There is a strong element of irony in the prospect that a compliance officer might be forced to veto incoming compliance demands because they are impossible to achieve, unreasonably costly, or allocate risk unfairly: no one wants to be ridiculed as the compliance officer who "killed the deal because it required us to be *too compliant*." At a minimum, if the compliance officer does not have the final word on acceptance of P2P compliance terms, there should be a serious conversation about who owns the incremental risk of a compliance regime accepted on grounds of business necessity.

Managing P2P compliance responsibly and with consistency requires a protocol for handling both incoming demands and the company's requests of third parties (including those originated both by the company and as flow-downs). This should include cataloging standard acceptable and unacceptable provisions as well as triggers for escalated review (such as indemnity clauses); triage for the referral of issues to subject-matter-experts outside the compliance function, such as sustainability, business continuity, and information technology; identification of the stakes, including applicable contractual remedies, in each case; evaluation of alternative responses, such as negotiation of terms, proposing tailored remedies rather than negotiating the substantive obligations, seeking approval of one's own code as a substitute, etc.; assignment of each of these tasks to identified personnel; and a decision-making framework for "business necessity" exceptions.

Critical to all of this is clarity—in advance—as to the authority and reporting lines of the compliance officers involved. A robust protocol, developed and implemented with senior executive input and board support, can do much to create this clarity, and to reinforce the compliance officer's objectivity and independence in carrying out the mandated role.

A reasoned, organized and disciplined approach to the accelerating P2P compliance trend can impose a certain amount of order on our unruly adolescent. But the single most effective approach to a complex problem is to simplify the problem. P2P compliance needs to grow up.

Childhood's End: Towards a Mature P2P Compliance Regime

The corporate community has a collective stake in simplifying management of the P2P compliance process while retaining its best features and fostering widespread acceptance of compliance cooperation and accountability throughout the value chain. Every company bears unnecessary costs stemming from the heterogeneity of P2P demands, the vanishing distinction between code and contract, the unprincipled attempts at risk transfer, and the administrative and operational burdens of sorting through, negotiating, and keeping track of all the commitments and seeing to their implementation.[37] Any company, at any given time, can find itself subjected to unreasonable demands from a trading partner possessed of superior bargaining power and a self-serving agenda. Any company may experience competing demands from opposite ends of its value chain, and every company will find it impossible to flow down everyone else's standards *ad infinitum*, in both directions. We need to develop a consensus on generally accepted principles of P2P compliance.

The companies least vulnerable to unfair pressures, and most able to inflict them, are our largest and most powerful enterprises. They should accept a leadership role in the effort to rationalize P2P compliance standards, and many of them have done so, singly as well as in groups such as the Electronic Industry Citizenship Coalition, the Pharmaceutical Supply Chain Initiative,[38] and the Automotive Industry Action Group.[39] They recognize that increasing contractual demands produce diminishing practical returns and that, in the end, reputational risk cannot be delegated. And some, to their credit, simply take to heart their own Code of Conduct admonitions to treat suppliers and customers with fairness.

The goal of this effort should be to establish common expectations that are proportional, balanced, and sensitive to the particular risk profile of a given relationship. As one example of an avenue worth exploring, it would be useful to draw a principled distinction between what is the appropriate content of a P2P Code, what should instead be considered for inclusion in a commercial contract, and what kinds of remedies are appropriate for each. To minimize negotiation and complexity, P2P Codes should be principle-based, and should address issues that are subject to wide consensus and that apply to all business activities. Matters that are essentially ethical in nature should appear in codes, as should all aspirational encouragement of goals where success cannot be assured or a deadline assigned, and for initiatives with no well-defined end-point and no extrinsic mandate. For many P2P Code violations, especially those directed at compliance processes rather than outcomes, remedies should be focused on moving the other party towards compliance, correction of past non-compliance, or termination of the relationship.

By contrast to P2P Codes, contracts focus on very particular business goals; they are risk-based and highly sensitive to the details of the business context. They map a path to the defined

---

[37] To be fair, not every company bears these costs. Some bear the alternate and deferred cost of ignoring the issues, agreeing to whatever comes over the transom, and dealing with the consequences later.

[38] *See* note 34 supra.

[39] *See* Ben DiPietro, "Automakers Face 'Herculean' Task in Implementing Supply Chain Guidelines," Wall Street Journal Risk & Compliance Journal, May 28, 2014, available at http://blogs.wsj.com/riskandcompliance/2014/05/28/automakers-face-herculean-task-in-implementing-supply-chain-guidelines/ (registration required; visited June 9, 2014); and the Automotive Industry Guiding Principles to Enhance Sustainability Performance in the Supply Chain, available at http://www.aiag.org/staticcontent/files/CorporateResponsibilityGuidanceStatements.pdf (visited June 9, 2014).

goals and seek to further each party's legitimate interests under the factual variations most likely to arise. Hence compliance provisions that relate specifically to the particular parties, to their specific goals, to the relevant market, and to the risks inherent in each should go into the contract where they can be negotiated in the light of those specific goals and risks, and appropriately targeted remedies can be assigned.

Collective action has been, and will continue to be, an important element in convening a consensus on P2P Code and contract content, but the foundation of true consensus will be the discrete but parallel decisions made by countless individual participants in light of their broader, long-term interests. These interests must be judged in the light of the company's dual role as both recipient and originator of compliance demands. Rather than having one code it imposes to protect itself and another set of principles that it is willing to be held accountable for, companies should develop a single, consistent portfolio of Golden Rule third-party commitments that it will accept as both obligor and beneficiary.[40] An essential companion effort, of course, is ensuring that one's compliance and ethics program and corporate social responsibility functions are up to the task of fulfilling these commitments. In the end, the goal is alignment among legal mandates, compliance program elements, and P2P commitments in both directions.

There will always be zero-sum business partners whose prime goal is risk transfer and who will do everything within their power to achieve it through contracts and P2P Codes. The tendency of standard-form documents to always grow, never shrink, and tilt ever more to one side is also well-known, and is trenchantly illustrated by the contractual creep of some companies' P2P codes. But the opposite can occur, and the proof is the dramatic evolution of internal corporate codes of conduct over the past several years. Fueled by a consensus about driving key values home, sticking to the main points, and leaving the details to other documents that can be consulted and applied when needed, corporate codes have become shorter, clearer, less adversarial and more digestible and memorable. With the right consensus within the business community, we can achieve the same new paradigm with P2P Codes. Let's get started.

---

[40] One of the most common responses to P2P Codes today is to trot out one's own code, indicating that it is substantially equivalent to the other party's proposed code, and offering to be bound by its conditions—and a few existing P2P codes expressly provide that the counterparty's code may be acceptable, especially for use in imposing flow-down requirements, if it is substantially equivalent to the first party's. When feasible, this process greatly simplifies administration; and converging standards of P2P Code content will facilitate its use.

Compliance & Ethics as a Profession—In the Public Interest

Joseph Murphy, Director of Public Policy
Society of Corporate Compliance and Ethics

I. Introduction

The field of compliance and ethics (C&E) is fairly described as a relatively new development. Compared to other areas of professional practice such as law and medicine, its pedigree is of recent vintage. There are many who would date it from the introduction of the US Organizational Sentencing Guidelines[1] in 1991(Sentencing Guidelines), although elements of the field predate that milestone.

Since the promulgation of the Sentencing Guidelines, many other standards and guidances for effective organizational compliance programs have been published. These include the Joint DOJ/SEC *Resource Guide to the U.S. Foreign Corrupt Practices Act*,[2] and outside the U.S., the OECD *Good Practice Guidance for Internal Controls, Ethics and Compliance*,[3] the UK Sentencing Council *Fraud, Bribery and Money Laundering: Corporate Offenders Definitive Guideline*,[4] the UK Ministry of Justice *Bribery Act 2010 Guidance*,[5] the Competition Commission of India *Competition Compliance Programme for Enterprises*,[6] and the Canadian Competition Bureau *Corporate Compliance Programs Bulletin*[7]—to name just a few. All of these sets of guidelines and standards, in response to an ever-expanding patchwork of laws and regulations on compliance, have brought more and more C&E practitioners into the field. The expansion of related law and guidance has added complexity and richness to C&E as a discipline and has contributed to its evolution into a vibrant, dynamic and multifaceted profession.

---

[1] U.S.S.G. section 8B2.1.

[2] US Department of Justice and US Securities and Exchange Commission, FCPA: A Resource Guide to the US Foreign Corrupt Practices Act (Nov. 14, 2012), http://www.justice.gov/criminal/fraud/fcpa/guide.pdf (visited June 9, 2014).

[3] Good Practice Guidance on Internal Controls, Ethics, and Compliance, available at http://www.oecd.org/investment/anti-bribery/anti-briberyconvention/44884389.pdf (visited June 9, 2014).

[4] http://sentencingcouncil.judiciary.gov.uk/docs/Fraud_bribery_and_money_laundering_offences_-_Definitive_guideline.pdf

[5] UK Ministry of Justice, The Bribery Act 2010, available at https://www.gov.uk/government/uploads/system/uploads/attachment_data/file/181762/bribery-act-2010-guidance.pdf (visited June 9, 2014).

[6] Competition Commission of India, Competition Compliance Programme for Enterprises. Available at http://www.cci.gov.in/images/media/Advocacy/comp_compliance_pro.pdf?phpMyAdmin=NMPFRahGKYeum5F74Ppstn7Rf00 (visited June 9, 2014).

[7] Canada Competition Bureau, Corporate Compliance Programs, available at http://www.competitionbureau.gc.ca/eic/site/cb-bc.nsf/eng/03280.html (visited June 9, 2014).

Along with the exponential growth of compliance and ethics as a profession, a wide spectrum of specialties and sub-specialties has evolved in response to the needs of specific industries and risk areas, such as privacy in the health care arena, or anti-money laundering in financial services. But some basic generalizations are instructive as we analyze this new profession.

The history of compliance and ethics logically parallels the growth in importance of large organizations in modern society. The field is about the prevention and detection of misconduct within organizations. It is also strikingly multidisciplinary. In order to control the conduct of large organizations and the multitude of employees and agents they may encompass, a broad range of management tools is required. But the field is not just the mechanical application of management tools; it also comes with an important mission. Its focus is to protect not just the organization, but society in general from the enormous harm that large organizations can inflict. Thus, C&E is a field with a mission.

Accompanying these historic developments are questions about the best way for C&E to proceed, not only as an effective function within organizations, but also as a professional discipline. Who should be doing the work? Who should have ultimate C&E responsibility in the organization? What are the respective responsibilities of the Board, management and the chief compliance officer? Are there fundamental principles in C&E, or is it a freewheeling exercise where each organization re-invents approaches? What role should government be playing? And related to all of these questions, what should the compliance field, and those who practice within it, be doing to further develop it as a new, evolving profession?

II. What Is This Field and Who Is in It?

As noted above, the field of compliance and ethics deals with methods within organizations to prevent and detect misconduct. This includes addressing all forms of illegal conduct attributable to the organization. This list is quite long, from antitrust to employment discrimination to environmental violations. The field also encompasses the prevention and detection of unethical conduct, beyond what is prescribed by law. In part, this reflects the recognition that any organization that is accustomed to cutting corners and engaging in sharp practices will also eventually run afoul of the law.

To achieve these objectives, the practitioners of C&E apply fundamental management principles used more broadly to achieve results in organizations. In the past there have been those who misperceived the field as being limited to policies, such as codes of conduct, and training. But for a compliance and ethics program to have any meaningful effect, it is necessary to use *all* the management techniques, tools and processes that organizations use when they want to achieve an important objective.

The model template for a compliance and ethics program is set out in the US Organizational Sentencing Guidelines,[8] widely followed as the most comprehensive framework for developing

[8] U.S.S.G. section 8B2.1.

an effective compliance program. While there are a number of other guides and standards on compliance programs as discussed above, the Sentencing Guidelines are the broadest in terms of scope, covering all types of violations, and incorporating a good mix of management steps to empower a meaningful compliance program. These steps include risk assessment, management responsibility, the setting of standards, imposition of internal controls, care in giving people responsibility, effective communications, meaningful discipline, appropriate incentives, audits and monitoring, evaluation of the compliance program, and mechanisms for people to raise compliance issues, and for investigating violations.

As would be expected given this range of steps, the types of positions in the C&E field are also broad and multidisciplinary. At the apex would be the chief ethics and compliance officer (CECO), responsible for the design and management of the program. There also need to be people with the ability to handle training, communications, audits, investigations, discipline, incentives, risk and program assessment, information technology and various other functions.

What draws all of this together, however, is the common mission and ethical positioning. The mission of C&E practitioners is to prevent and detect misconduct by the organization and all those acting for it. While practitioners in this field have an employer, they also have a singular duty to protect the public, operating in an environment where they may be the first to know of incipient harm. Unlike others in the organization, this is not a sidelight of their job; this is their entire job.

III. What Is Meant by C&E as a "Profession"?

Given the new and evolving nature of this field, some ask: is it, or should it be, a profession? Here we will examine briefly the general characteristics of a profession, and the progress of the compliance and ethics field against these criteria.

Perhaps the most distinctive aspect of the field, and a key characteristic of any profession, is its nexus to the public interest. The focus on preventing organizational crime and other violations goes to the core of public concerns. Those who practice in the C&E field have a duty well beyond the four walls of their employer. While there is certainly a duty to one's employer to advance its interests, the duty to prevent and detect misconduct is not just part of this field; it is the reason—as noted in the Sentencing Guidelines—that it exists.

Professions are also noted for their specialized knowledge and training. Over the last 20+ years, the modern compliance and ethics field has developed a broad spectrum of specialized skills, knowledge and practices necessary to discharge the evolving mandate to detect and prevent corporate misconduct. These skills and practices include necessary management elements—the ability to motivate people and to explain the rules, knowledge of how to conduct investigations and audits, and ability to measure and monitor progress against goals, to name a few. But the field also has its own prescriptive standards, as first embodied and codified by the Sentencing Guidelines. Different jurisdictions and different enforcement agencies provide additional guidance, and practitioners need to understand and master these.

The development of the specialized mandate, knowledge, and skills in the field is also reflected in the establishment of several professional organizations supporting the training and sharing of best practices by C&E practitioners, including the Society of Corporate Compliance and Ethics, the Ethics and Compliance Officer Association, and the Australasian Compliance Institute,[9] and also industry specific groups such as the Health Care Compliance Association and the Securities Industry and Financial Markets Association. In a somewhat related vein, an increasing number of colleges, universities[10] and graduate schools have developed courses and, in some cases, degree programs in the field of compliance and ethics.

Parallel to the development of the field's specific mandate, knowledge and skills has been a strong momentum for an independent compliance function that is elevated and empowered within the organization. Although historically many companies tended to subordinate their compliance and ethics departments within the general counsel's office, elevating the CECO to executive status, and to serving as an independent voice in the C-Suite, has become an increasingly prevalent trend.[11]

Apart from the growing stature of the CECO, the codified body of compliance standards, and the emergence of multiple professional societies in C&E, there have also been several other developments that signify the evolution of the C&E field toward professional status. For example, the ethical dimension of the field is also becoming more standardized, in a way that demands mastery by those entering the field. Again, formal standards around a central body of knowledge and practice are a core element of any profession. With regard to ethical standards for those practicing in the C&E field, the Code of Professional Ethics promulgated by the Society of Corporate Compliance and Ethics provides detailed rules and commentary that give important guidance for those operating in the field.[12]

Professions also are identified with autonomy and a shared experience. In no field is autonomy more important for the benefit of society than it is in C&E. A compliance and ethics practitioner works in organizations surrounded by hundreds or thousands of colleagues. These colleagues are all part of the "team," with a goal to advance the organization's interests. The compliance and ethics person, by contrast, is ethically compelled to stand up to the group and the team. While others may go along with the team, or may be allowed simply to give advice and

---

[9] Subsequently redesignated the "GRC Institute."

[10] For example, The New England College of Business offers a Masters Degree in Business Ethics and Compliance, http://www.necb.edu/master-of-science-in-business-ethics-and-compliance-online.cfm (visited June 9, 2014) and the University of St. Thomas School of Law in St. Paul, MN, offers a Masters and LLM degree in Organizational Compliance and Ethics, http://www.stthomas.edu/law/compliance/ (visited June 9, 2014).

[11] While the debate on the positioning and independence of compliance continues, at least one recent study suggests that compliance programs led by individuals reporting to the CEO, the Board, or an independent Board committee—instead of to the general counsel—are significantly more effective. LRN 2014 Ethics and Compliance Program Effectiveness Report, available at http://pages.lrn.com/the-2014-ethics-and-compliance-program-effectiveness-report (visited June 9, 2014).

[12] Code of Professional Ethics for Compliance and Ethics Professionals, available at http://corporatecompliance.org/Resources/View/smid/940/ArticleID/675.aspx (visited June 9, 2014).

leave the decisions to the team, a compliance and ethics person does not have that option. Rather, he or she must use whatever steps are necessary to prevent misconduct.[13] This is an enormously difficult role, and it calls for the person to stand independent and autonomous.

The other half of this separateness is that it creates a shared experience among all those dedicated to the compliance and ethics mission. When their corporate teammates may scorn them for being the only ones not going along with the plan, the compliance and ethics person can reach out and network with other peers who have experienced this same resistance. The professional associations supporting C&E practitioners provide a wide range of opportunities for facilitating this shared experience via best practice sharing and networking. More recently, a vibrant and evolving panoply of social media outlets has added exponentially to this process.

Professions are also associated with self-regulation. They set standards for their members and then require their members to adhere to those standards. They also require practitioners to demonstrate a high level of competence to enter and remain in the field. Members of the profession band together to develop and administer the standards, and to provide a system for promoting professionalism.

In the compliance and ethics field this process has been developing. The Society of Corporate Compliance and Ethics has developed a strong Code of Professional Ethics for Compliance and Ethics Professionals. It has also gone through the long and detailed process to develop a certification system.[14] Today, those in the field can obtain the status of Certified Compliance and Ethics Professional through meeting the educational requirements and then satisfactorily completing an exam. For example, as of this writing, there are approximately 7,000 practitioners with this and related C&E certifications.[15]

One remaining issue in the professionalization of C&E, however, is the role of the government in the process. In order for a membership organization to police its members' competence and ethical performance, it is necessary to consider the role of government. Without government support, it is highly problematical for any membership organization to impose sanctions against those pursuing their careers. The risks in the legal environment are enormous, and without the government playing a role, the membership organization has little if any power to impose meaningful sanctions. A remaining issue, then, is whether there is a role for the government in supporting professional certification in C&E, and providing protection for those called upon to police the field.[16]

---

[13] Code of Professional Ethics for Compliance and Ethics Professionals.

[14] Compliance Certification Board, available at http://www.compliancecertification.org/AboutCCB/EarningCCBaccreditation/Programaccreditation.aspx (visited June 9, 2014).

[15] The Compliance Certification Board of the SCCE/HCCA currently offers seven types of certification to compliance professionals, http://www.compliancecertification.org/CCEP/CertifiedComplianceEthicsProfessional.aspx (visited June 9, 2014).

[16] Obviously and by analogy to established professions including law and medicine, government is often involved in backing those professions through a formal licensing framework, thereby ensuring substantial professional

IV. The Public Interest and the Need for Professionalism

In the fields that have traditionally been considered professions, there is certainly a public interest in their status. In medicine, for example, the average citizen cannot be expected to understand the intricacies of the medical field, yet the health of the population is clearly a matter of public interest. Yes, most medicine may be mundane, but all citizens face the prospect of medical emergencies where they are at the mercy of the medical practitioner. Thus, the public wants to be sure of the quality and integrity of the providers.

Similarly in the practice of law, most of the services may be routine, but the chance that one may face a legal tribunal or a powerful prosecutor leads society to value a system that ensures the integrity, competence and loyalty of the legal profession.

In this light, consider the remarkable role of the compliance and ethics practitioner. The C&E person spends his or her entire day working to prevent conduct that by definition imperils the public. Picture the compliance person in a pharmaceutical company, for example. While one rogue doctor might harm dozens or possibly hundreds of individuals, one rogue pharmaceutical product could hurt millions of people around the world. Picture the compliance person working in a chemical company. One bad lawyer might cause innocent individuals to lose cases or be unfairly incarcerated, but one bad control system could lead to a disaster like Bhopal.

The defining point here is the degree of potential harm that can come from organizational misconduct, and the demonstrated inability of the state to do anything more than come in after the disaster and try to allocate blame. One of the most important elements of modern society is the growth of large organizations. In a world where markets now span the globe, businesses operate on a massive scale. But it is not only industry where this occurs. Universities, governments, charities, and other non-governmental organizations—all have become larger and more pervasive.[17]

With this increase in size and scope has come an increased ability to impact society. The degree of potential harm from such large organizations is striking. Unfortunately, equally noteworthy is the inability of any organization outside of such large entities to control their conduct. Even a casual observer must be impressed by the steady parade of stories of significant organizational crime and misconduct. While each major business crime is followed by stories of investigations, outrage and public fulminations, the denouement is typically the simple transfer of funds from large companies to large governments, and the occasional sacrifice of a few

---

autonomy and self-governance, but also with a formal disciplinary acknowledgment of public responsibility, as well as for standard setting and enforcement. It is an open question whether, or in what manner, these sorts of professional licensing models can or should apply, in the context of C&E as an emerging professional discipline.

[17] For example, the Rutgers Center for Government Compliance and Ethics (where the author serves as Chairman of the Advisory Board) has as its mission the encouragement of compliance and ethics programs as an element of public governance at the federal, state, and local levels in the United States and worldwide through a variety of activities including research, education, networking, and thought leadership, available at http://rcgce.camlaw.rutgers.edu (visited June 9, 2014).

employees in a public trial. But none of this process seems to interdict the crime before the harm is done.

The one exception to this process is the development of a strong internal force to stop corporate crime and misconduct before the harm is done. This is the essential role of compliance and ethics practitioners within the organization. Yet these practitioners are potentially in the most vulnerable position imaginable—always outnumbered by peers who are well into the groupthink that leads to organizational misadventures. The compliance and ethics person is called upon to stand up for a public that often does not even know the person exists. Given this circumstance, a strong, even compelling, argument exists that the compliance and ethics practitioner has a greater need to be considered a profession than do many of the other established professions.

If the compliance and ethics person is to be the bulwark against so many dangerous forms of misconduct and entrenched power structures, then there needs to be more than a fond hope that this he or she can play this role in an effective way. There is urgent need for this essential position to be strengthened in meaningful ways. Placing these practitioners in the role of professionals is a major step along this path.

V. How a Strong Professional Ethical Standard Can Help

Among the most important sources of support a compliance and ethics practitioner can have is a strong and specific code of professional ethics. This is especially important in a corporate environment where loyalty is highly prized, and failure to go along with the corporate team is considered suspect. When an employee is empowered to refuse to conform to the corporate group's demands, because of a specific mandate from his or her profession, this can be a powerful event.

For example, in the corporate world the usual rule is that one's boss makes the final call on things. So if a compliance person says a certain course violates the company's code of conduct, but the boss nevertheless wants to do it (and the lawyers advise it is not illegal), what does the compliance person do? Under SCCE's code of ethics there is no ambiguity. The compliance person must take whatever steps are necessary to prevent the violation. This is not merely a requirement to give competent advice; it is a call for action. When the boss says, "enough, I have decided," the compliance person then has no option; the person must escalate the matter, all the way to the board of directors.[18]

If a compliance practitioner is asked to conduct an investigation as a result of a whistleblower's allegations, but is told not to go too far and not to bother certain managers who are too busy to be interrupted, the compliance practitioner again has no choice.[19] He or she must

---

[18] Code of Professional Ethics for Compliance and Ethics Professionals, R 1.2, R 1.4, available at http://corporatecompliance.org/Resources/View/smid/940/ArticleID/675.aspx (visited June 9, 2014).

[19] Compare with the report by the Pulitzer Prize winning New York Times author David Barstow in the Wal-Mart Mexican bribery case that investigators were criticized by the CEO for being too "aggressive,"

insist on conducting a diligent investigation consistent with professional standards. If this is not permitted, then the compliance and ethics person must advise the board, including details relating to the circumstances.[20]

In the corporate world, one can express opinions, but usually when the boss says "march," the only questions left are "how far and how fast." The compliance and ethics person, though, is charged with a duty that history has shown few if any in the corporate world have been willing or able to do. When the answer should be "no," the compliance and ethics person must say "no." Without the power that comes from being a professional, in today's environment the compliance and ethics practitioner is simply being set up to fail.

VI. Going Forward

What can we do going forward to further support the development of the compliance and ethics profession? Those of us in the C&E field can pay more attention to developing a common ethical code such as the SCCE Code of Professional Ethics. This includes:

- Making it part of employment contracts
- Making it part of position descriptions
- Incorporating it into company compliance and ethics programs, e.g., in board resolutions and policies on the program
- Referring to it whenever it covers issues we are addressing in our work
- Including it in our writings and presentations when dealing with our field

We must also promote the professionalization of the field. For example, companies can specify that professional certification, like the CCEP, is a job preference or requirement when hiring for positions in compliance and ethics. Professionalism is supported when compliance officers are recruited and hired based upon their professional qualifications and experience in compliance and ethics, and not based upon flashy credentials in other fields like litigation and enforcement.

We in the compliance and ethics profession should also take charge of defining our own field and its requirements. Gone are the days when others who have never practiced in the field should be speaking for, or defining, the profession. This may have been more routine in the early stages of the field, but 20+ years of robust, in-depth practice and experience have elevated the profession from the back office to the C-Suite, with the maturity to define its own future.

The profession should also continue to develop and scrutinize educational and training opportunities for compliance and ethics practitioners. For instance, as colleges, universities and graduate schools develop formal curricula in response to the demand for skilled professionals,

---

http://www.nytimes.com/2012/04/22/business/at-wal-mart-in-mexico-a-bribe-inquiry-silenced.html?pagewanted=all&_r=0 (visited June 9, 2014).

[20] Code of Professional Ethics for Compliance and Ethics Professionals, R 3.1 & Commentary, available at http://corporatecompliance.org/Resources/View/smid/940/ArticleID/675.aspx (visited June 9, 2014).

the field should advise and have input into those efforts, to ensure that relevant skills and knowledge reflecting practical experience are incorporated.

Much thought is being given these days to the protection of whistleblowers, usually meaning those who object to illegal activity. But the OECD Working Group on Bribery very quietly hit a point that few have yet noticed. In the OECD's Good Practice Guidance on compliance programs, the provision on preventing retaliation included the following:

> 11. effective measures for:
>
> . . .
>
> ii) internal and where possible confidential reporting by, and protection of, directors, officers, employees, and, where appropriate, business partners, *not willing to violate professional standards or ethics* under instructions or pressure from hierarchical superiors, as well as for directors, officers, employees, and, where appropriate, business partners, *willing to report breaches of* the law or *professional standards or ethics* occurring within the company, in good faith and on reasonable grounds; . . . (emphasis added)[21]

Protection should also be offered for those who stand by their professional standards as well. Companies could readily modify their codes of conduct and compliance program standards to prohibit retaliation against those unwilling to violate professional standards, including the standards for compliance and ethics professionals. Governments, in turn, could apply this same standard for laws and regulations providing protection against retaliation.

The government could strengthen compliance and ethics programs by joining the effort to professionalize the field. When monitors are appointed and compliance programs are required as part of case resolutions, governments can indicate their preference for professional status in monitors, compliance officers, etc., and especially by requiring conformity to a tough professional code like that used by the SCCE.

Finally, there is the issue of professional accountability. There is value in having a system for holding professionals accountable for their conduct, based on the professional code of ethics. For this to happen there should be support from the state, so that the profession can do this effectively. At least some form of immunity would be appropriate if members of the profession are to take on this often-onerous task.

The development of the compliance and ethics field as a profession is new and evolving. As is likely the case for any new idea, there is ongoing opposition from those with vested interests in the current system

But the public's interest in preventing the great harm organizations can and do cause needs to be paramount. Those courageous individuals charged with this high-tension and often perilous task need more than platitudes to achieve their objective. If society is to ask these individuals to

---

[21] OECD, Recommendation of the Council for Further Combating Bribery of Foreign Public Officials in International Business Transactions, Appendix II, available at http://www.oecd.org/daf/anti-bribery/44884389.pdf

stand up to the force of determined power in organizations, then it needs to equip them to do the job.

Those in the compliance and ethics field have shown great resolve in forming and driving their profession. And that profession is rapidly expanding and responding to the needs of organizations. But there is more work to be done to further develop the field.

It is not every day we witness the birth of a new profession. The development of the compliance and ethics profession is undeniably critical to the public interest and requires the support and attention of government, policymakers, the academic community, and all other stakeholders with an interest in strong and effective self-governance programs in organizations.

Redefining the Relationship of the General Counsel and Chief Compliance Officer[1]

Michael Volkov, CEO
The Volkov Law Group

"Change is the law of life. And those who look only to the past or present are certain to miss the future."
—John F. Kennedy

I. The Independent Chief Compliance Officer Versus the General Counsel

Change is hard to accept for those who are looking to the past. We are all guilty, at one point or another, of resisting change. Such resistance, however, usually gives way to evident improvements that directly result from change. In the end, we all learn an important lesson in life—change can be good.

Over the last ten years, there has been a sea change in the positioning and responsibilities of Chief Compliance Officers (CCOs). CCOs are being elevated in the corporate governance world to assume increasing responsibilities and carry new burdens. At the same time, corporate leaders are empowering CCOs and compliance professionals as independent forces within the company.[2]

The independent, empowered CCO is favored by many corporate governance experts, compliance experts, the United States Sentencing Commission, federal prosecutors and regulators and numerous studies which support the proposition that separation of the compliance

---

[1] [Editor's note: The discussion in this white paper refers extensively to the case of *Barko v Halliburton*, No. 1:05-cv-1276 (DDC Mar. 6, 2014). Following the date of the RAND symposium event and the writing of this paper, the U.S. Court of Appeals for the DC Circuit overturned the judgment of the lower court, and ruled that Halliburton's internal investigation fell within the scope of attorney-client privilege. See *In re: Kellogg, Brown & Root*, 2014 WL 2895939 (CADC June 27, 2014).]

[2] The 2013 PWC State of Compliance Survey highlights, among other trends, that CCOs are "gaining clout" in the C-Suite, with the percentage of CCOs reporting to the CEO in the US increasing to 28%, up 8% from 2012. At the same time, the number of CCOs reporting to the General Counsel (32%) continued its downward trend, down 3% from 2012 and a total of 9% from 2011. Compare PWC State of Compliance 2013 Survey, available at http://www.pwc.com/us/en/risk-management/2013-state-compliance-survey.jhtml (visited June 9, 2014) (32 percent of CCOs formally report to General Counsel [UK and US based companies]); PWC States of Compliance 2012 Survey, available at http://www.pwc.com/us/en/risk-management/2012-state-compliance-survey.jhtml (visited June 9, 2014) (35 percent of CCOs formally report to General Counsel); and PWC State of Compliance 2011 Survey, available at http://www.pwc.com/en_US/us/risk-management/assets/MW-11-0297_Compliance_Week_final.pdf (visited June 9, 2014) (41 percent of CCOs formally report to General Counsel); Association of Corporate Counsel and Corpedia, Benchmarking Survey on Compliance Programs and Risk Assessments, available at http://www.acc.com/legalresources/resource.cfm?show=1350989 (visited June 9, 2014) (39 percent of CCOs reporting to CEO).

function from legal is a best practice and one that should be encouraged by everyone in the governance field.[3]

The momentum for CCO independence is further validated by a new LRN research study on compliance program effectiveness that found:

> Programs led by an individual reporting to either the CEO or the board (or one of its committees) substantially outperform those reporting to the general counsel.[4]

This trend is not in response to an aggressive enforcement environment. The message behind compliance has finally been heard—effective ethics and compliance programs contribute to the bottom line by increasing profits and enhancing sustainable growth.[5] A key ingredient for an "effective" ethics and compliance program is an independent and empowered CCO.[6]

For years before this current trend, CCOs were reporting to the General Counsel and classified as a portion of the corporate legal department. Those days are gone.

Annual survey information confirms what we already know—companies are extricating CCOs from the legal department, elevating them to senior management positions, clarifying their separate mandate, and having them report to the CEO or other top executives. Along with this new position, companies are finally increasing resources to the compliance function to manage

---

[3] Survey conducted by Society for Corporate Compliance and Ethics and Health Care Compliance Association, March 11, 2013, available at http://www.corporatecompliance.org/Resources/View/ArticleId/918/Compliance-professionals-overwhelmingly-reject-general-counsel-reporting-structure.aspx (visited June 9, 2014); http://www.corporatecompliance.org/Login.aspx?returnurl=%2fResources%2fView%2fArticleId%2f909%2fShould-Compliance-Report-to-the-General-Counsel.aspx (finding that 88 percent of compliance professionals oppose General Counsel also serving as chief compliance officer); Keshav Nair, Brave New World for the CCO, The Network GRC Blog, January 8, 2013, available at http://www.tnwinc.com/index.php/blog/comments/brave_cco (visited June 9, 2014); The Business Case for Creating a Standalone Chief Compliance Officer Position, Ethisphere, available at http://m1.ethisphere.com/resources/whitepaper-separation-of-General Counsel-and-cco.pdf (visited June 9, 2014); GRC: The Evolution Chief Ethics and Compliance Officer Role, Scott Giordano, CMS Wire, June 9, 2011, available at http://www.cmswire.com/cms/information-management/grc-the-evolution-chief-ethics-and-compliance-officer-role-011557.php (visited June 9, 2014); Jacelyn Jaeger, The Importance of Splitting Legal and Compliance, Compliance Week, December 2011, available at http://www.mwe.com/info/pubs/splitting_legal_and_compliance.pdf (visited June 9, 2014); Jose Tabuena, The Chief Compliance Officer vs. the General Counsel: Friend or Foe? Compliance & Ethics Magazine, December 2006, available at http://www.corporatecompliance.org/Portals/1/PDF/Resources/past_handouts/CEI/2008/601-3.pdf (visited June 9, 2014); Health Care Compliance Officer and Legal Counsel Relationships, Health Law Blog, Feb. 20, 2011, available at http://www.healthlaw-blog.com/2011/02/compliance-officer-and-legal-counsel-dual-role/ (visited June 9, 2014); An Integrated Approach to Corporate Compliance, Department of Health and Human Services and American Health Lawyers Association, July 1, 2004, available at https://oig.hhs.gov/fraud/docs/complianceguidance/Tab%204E%20Appendx-Final.pdf (visited June 9, 2014).

[4] The 2014 Ethics and Compliance Program Effectiveness Report is described by LRN as "the first serious, comprehensive analysis of 'program effectiveness' in terms of its impact on the behaviors and attitudes that make up organizational culture," http://pages.lrn.com/the-2014-ethics-and-compliance-program-effectiveness-report (visited June 9, 2014).

[5] *See* Simon Webley and Elise More, Does Business Ethics Pay, Institute of Business Ethics (2003), available at http://www.ibe.org.uk/userfiles/doesbusethicpaysumm.pdf (visited June 9, 2014).

[6] An Independent CCO is a Compliance Program Requirement, available at http://corruptioncrimecompliance.com/2013/04/an-independent-cco-is-a-compliance-program-requirement/ (visited June 9, 2014).

the enormous and often perilous job of preventing and detecting misconduct within the organization.[7]

The survey information also confirms public reports by many major companies that have elevated and separated CCOs from the legal function in the financial, oil and gas, health care and retail industries, among others. Some of these changes have been adopted in response to government enforcement actions but some have not. The list of high-profile companies includes: Wal-Mart,[8] HSBC,[9] J.P. Morgan,[10] Goldman Sachs,[11] Barclays, UBS, Gap, Parker Drilling, and a long line of companies in the health care industry such as Pfizer,[12] Johnson & Johnson, Eli Lilly and Merck.

For General Counsels, the elevation of the CCO has brought about change in their own responsibilities and roles. Many often forget that, over the last few decades, General Counsels have seen their own stock rise in the corporate governance marketplace—gone are the days when General Counsels sat in an office opining on legal issues to keep the company in compliance with the law. Instead, General Counsels have taken on a greater business role in the company. CEOs often rely on their General Counsel for more than just "legal" advice and seek guidance on "business" issues.

Even with this significant change in the respective roles of the CCO and the General Counsel, there are some who resist this movement. Some General Counsels long for the old days

---

[7] Thomson Reuters Cost of Compliance 2014, available at http://accelus.thomsonreuters.com/sites/default/files/GRC00814.pdf (visited June 9, 2014); SAI Global 2013 C&E Benchmarking Survey, available at http://compliance.saiglobal.com/assets/whitepapers/SAI-GLOBAL-whitepaper-2013-global-ce-benchmarking-survey.pdf (visited June 9, 2014); Deloitte's Compliance Trends Survey 2013, available at http://www.deloitte.com/view/en_US/us/Services/audit-enterprise-risk-services/governance-regulatory-risk-strategies/Regulatory-Compliance-Services/256ad7d579d50410VgnVCM3000003456f70aRCRD.htm (visited June 9, 2014).

[8] *See* Wal-Mart Global Compliance Program Report http://corporate.walmart.com/global-responsibility/global-compliance-program-report-on-fiscal-year-2014; Matt Kelly, Walmart Outlines Compliance Reforms, April 23, 2014, available at http://www.complianceweek.com/walmart-outlines-compliance-reforms-part-i/article/343986/ (visited June 9, 2014).

[9] Rachel Ensign, HSBC Confirms Compliance Reorganization, Wall Street Journal, November 15, 2013, available at http://blogs.wsj.com/riskandcompliance/2013/11/15/hsbc-confirms-compliance-reorganization/ (visited June 9, 2014); Boehme, Donna, DOJ Tells HSBC and Corporate America: Reform Your Compliance Departments, Corporate Counsel, December 20, 2012, available at http://compliancestrategists.com/csblog/2012/12/20/doj-tells-hsbc-corporate-america-reform-compliance-departments/ (visited June 9, 2014).

[10] Donna Boehme and Michael Volkov, J.P. Morgan Chase Takes a Giant Step on CCO Independence, Corporate Counsel, January 29, 2013, available at http://compliancestrategists.com/csblog/wp-content/uploads/2013/11/ Corporate-Counsel_-JPMorgan-Chase-Takes-a-Giant-Step-on-CCO-Independence.pdf (visited June 9, 2014).

[11] Donna Boehme, Big Banks Giving the CCO a Seat at the Table, Corporate Counsel, March 1, 2013, available at http://compliancestrategists.com/csblog/wp-content/uploads/2013/11/Corporate-Counsel_-Big-Banks-Giving-the-CCO-a-Seat-at-the-Table.pdf (visited June 9, 2014).

[12] See Pfizer settlement, available at http://www.oig.hhs.gov/fraud/cia/agreements/pfizer_inc.pdf (visited June 9, 2014); Amy Miller, Going With Plan B: Pfizer GC No Longer Oversees Compliance, Corporate Counsel (September 10, 2009), available at http://www.law.com/jsp/article.jsp?id=1202433692974&Going_With_Plan_B_Pfizer_GC_No_Longer_Oversees_Compliance&slreturn=20130229164233 (visited June 9, 2014).

when they controlled the CCO, and when they ultimately were responsible for the design and implementation of the company's ethics and compliance program. Some General Counsels have resisted the elevation of the CCO as a direct threat to their own interests. This resistance can take many forms, some of which merely reflect intra-company squabbles and politics. Some of the controversy may arise from an imperfect understanding of the modern mandate of the CCO beyond mere "compliance with laws"—a mandate that may from time to time conflict with that of the GC.[13] Other arguments raised by General Counsels, however, have started to galvanize some in the General Counsel community, and powerful business lobbying and advocacy groups, and center on a perceived threat to a basic corporate protection—the attorney-client privilege.

As explained in this white paper, the rise of the CCO and ethics and compliance programs is neither a threat to the attorney-client privilege, nor to the corporate standing of General Counsels. To the contrary, a General Counsel and a CCO need each other even more than ever to reinforce and enhance the ultimate success of the legal function, the ethics and compliance program, and the organization itself.

In this context, it is interesting to watch how legal professionals and powerful business and legal advocacy groups are using the issue of attorney-client privilege to suggest that CCOs, or the compliance function, may operate in ways that undermine the ability of a corporation to preserve and maintain the attorney-client privilege.

This debate, which is now playing out in the appeal of the district court decision in *Harry Barko v. Halliburton*,[14] reflects a classic straw man concern that serves only to distract the courts, policymakers and legal and compliance professionals from beginning on a new and more important task: the realignment and redefinition of the respective roles of the independent CCO and the General Counsel, and the development of effective protocols for coordinating the legal and compliance functions.

Unlike those who argue that the sky is falling, and that the attorney-client privilege will forever be eviscerated, this white paper outlines a profound grasp of the obvious—the change in the respective roles of the CCO and the General Counsel require the CCO to define a new relationship designed to promote ethics and compliance while preserving and even enhancing important legal functions, including the attorney-client privilege, needed to ensure that legal advice can be given to the CCO or other executives, where appropriate.

II. The Importance of the Attorney-Client Privilege to Legal and Compliance Functions

The General Counsel is the guardian of legal risks, providing important guidance and functions needed for the company to ensure compliance with the law. A CCO builds on the company's legal compliance foundation, by promoting not only compliance with the law, but adherence to a

[13] Donna Boehme, When Compliance and Legal Don't See Eye-to-Eye, May 8, 2014, available at http://compliancestrategists.com/csblog/wp-content/uploads/2014/05/When-Compliance-and-Legal-Dont-See-Eye-to-Eye.pdf (visited June 9, 2014).

[14] No. 1:05-cv-1276 (D.D.C. Mar. 6, 2014).

culture of ethics and a specific business code of conduct—and by finding, fixing and remedying related problems.

One of the General Counsel's most important tools is the attorney-client privilege. It is the means by which the General Counsel encourages full and frank discussions with legal advisors to define legal boundaries, to learn of company operations and potential legal issues, and ultimately, it is a valuable means by which the General Counsel contributes to the company's efforts to detect and prevent legal violations.

A robust and effective attorney-client privilege is critical to a company's ability to detect and prevent potential violations of law. Company actors rely on the privilege as a way to encourage communications on legal issues, to provide sound legal advice, and to promote frank discussions of legal issues. In the absence of such protection, a company's legal officers would be unable to promote and ensure that the company conforms to the law.

The CCO is responsible for implementing and overseeing an effective ethics and compliance program. An effective ethics and compliance program is designed to be open and transparent to employees, management and the government. Companies promote transparency of their ethics and compliance programs to demonstrate strong self-governance, to build cultures of compliance, and to incentivize their employees to engage in the culture, and to come forward with issues that the company needs to address.

A simple analogy may help: the General Counsel defines the lanes in a road; and the CCO is responsible for processes and systems designed to ensure that the corporation stays within those lanes. The CCO should not draw its own lanes defining legal and illegal behavior—that is not the CCO's job. At the same time, the CCO is the independent subject matter expert concerning the broader compliance program, which encompasses much more than just the defined legal lanes.

Compliance officers need the attorney-client privilege for various functions. For example, a CCO's ability to identify potential violations of the law, have them investigated, and then design a remediation plan to fix the identified problem all depend on the ability of the CCO to operate in close coordination with the legal function, to preserve confidentiality and the attorney-client privilege while the company addresses these important issues.

On the other side of the equation, CCOs also need to conduct many of their critical functions outside the attorney-client privilege, including audits, monitoring hotlines and complaint processes, conduct of investigations of complaints, training, ethics communications, etc. The vibrancy of an ethics and compliance program depends on the ability of a CCO to communicate and disseminate important compliance values, policies and procedures.

In the end, a compliance program is only as good as it is embraced and embedded within the culture of a company. In this process, there is no room for blanket confidentiality, secrecy and claim of privilege.

III. Drawing the Lines between Compliance and Legal: Internal Investigations and the Attorney-Client Privilege

The boundary between the legal and compliance functions is tested in the handling of internal investigations. Every compliance program requires an internal investigation and discipline process to identify potential legal and code of conduct violations, and mete out discipline for violations of law and/or a code of conduct. Many companies have established internal investigation units, either as part of the auditing function or the compliance program.[15] Most of these internal investigation operations coordinate closely with the legal department to ensure that certain internal investigations are conducted under the privilege.

In recent years, litigation of attorney-client privilege claims has increased over access to internal investigation documents and reports. The stakes are high in these situations because disclosure of otherwise privileged documents creates significant litigation risks.

The issue of whether the attorney-client privilege or the work product doctrine applies to documents created as part of an internal compliance investigation is not new or novel.[16] Rather, as the Supreme Court stated in *Upjohn Co. v. United States*, the outcome in any particular circumstance must be determined on a "case-by-case basis" and depends on the particular circumstances of the case.[17]

On May 7, 2014, the D.C. Circuit heard an appeal of a *qui tam* whistleblower case *Barko v. Halliburton/KBR*, arising from allegations that KBR engaged in contract fraud in one of their major Iraqi war contracts. From all angles, this case appears to turn on a simple fact-based question of attorney-client privilege under federal law.

Yet the matter appears to have attracted a mountain of amicus briefs from the likes of the U.S. Chamber of Commerce, the Association of Corporate Counsel and the National Association of Manufacturers, all of which are worried about the ability of companies to conduct internal investigations under the cloak of the attorney-client privilege.

The facts of the case are straightforward. Former KBR employee Harry Barko reported fraud and contracting abuses he believed were committed by KBR in spending the monies it obtained from the U.S. government to pay costs associated with the war in Iraq. He was particularly concerned over KBR's practices in providing large subcontracts to a Jordanian company known as Daoud.

Mr. Barko used the internal reporting procedures established in KBR's Code of Business Conduct ("COBC") to report his allegations regarding the KBR-Daoud fraud. Consistent with

---

[15] United States Sentencing Guidelines, Section 8B2.1(b)(7).

[16] Upjohn Co. v. United States, 449 U.S. 383 (1981); Solis v. Food Emp'rs Labor Relations Ass'n, 644 F.3d 221 (4th Cir. 2011); Permian Corp. v. United States, 665 F.2d 1214 (D.C. Cir. 1981); Wultz v. Bank of China, Ltd., F. Supp. 2d ____, 2013 WL 5797114 (S.D.N.Y. Oct. 25, 2013); United States v. ISS Marine Servs., Inc., 905 F. Supp. 2d 121 (D.D.C. 2012); United States v. Dish Network, LLC, 283 F.R.D. 420 (N.D. Ill. 2012); In re Intel Corp. Microprocessor Antitrust Litig., 258 F.R.D. 280 (D. Del. 2008).

[17] Upjohn, 449 U.S. at 396.

the Code, KBR investigated Mr. Barko's allegations. The company then wrote up internal reports concerning the investigators findings, and thereafter hid the reports from public scrutiny. Nothing was reported to the federal government.

Fast forward approximately ten years later. Mr. Barko, frustrated by his belief that KBR hid evidence of fraud, filed a False Claims Act/*qui tam* legal action in an attempt to hold the company accountable. As part of his lawsuit he asked that KBR produce in discovery the COBC reports. KBR refused. They claimed that because an attorney managed the COBC program, the reports were privileged. Barko filed a motion to compel.

In response to Barko's motion the federal judge hearing the case reviewed the COBC reports *in camera*. The judge described the documents:

> The Court has reviewed KBR's COBC Reports and they are eye-openers. KBR's investigator found Daoud: "received preferential treatment." The reports include both direct and circumstantial evidence that Daoud paid off KBR employees and KBR employees steered business to Daoud. And the KBR investigation "reported a trend that D&P would routinely submit bids after proposals from other companies had been received." The reports suggest some KBR employee or employees fed information about competitor bids to Daoud to allow Daoud to submit a late bid undercutting the competitors. . . . The reports say Daoud continually received contracts despite terrible completion performance and despite regular attempts to double bill. In one case, KBR gave Daoud a contract despite Daoud's bid being twice another bid from a competent contractor.

On March 6, 2014, after conducting his *in camera* review, the judge ordered KBR to produce all of its COBC reports related to Mr. Barko's allegations.

The district judge explained that the "investigations were undertaken pursuant to regulatory law and corporate policy rather than for the purpose of obtaining legal advice." As a result, the trial judge determined that the investigation was of a "business nature" rather than a "legal nature."[18]

Significantly, the district court cited the fact that the KBR Code, as approved by the company, did not state that COBC investigations were confidential or covered under an attorney-client privilege. The Code provided a specific procedure for KBR to invoke an attorney-client privileged investigation. KBR failed to exercise this procedure in Mr. Barko's case.[19]

KBR's conducted the investigation without any attention to the attorney-client privilege. For example, KBR investigators failed to advise employees of basic rights as required under *Upjohn*. In addition, the employees who were interviewed were never told: (1) the purpose of the investigation; (2) that the investigation was being conducted under the attorney-client privilege; (3) that KBR retained the privilege and would decide whether or not to waive the privilege; or (4) that they were entitled to representation during the interview.

---

[18] *Order* at 5-8.

[19] Ibid.

Faced with the prospect of having to turn over the highly incriminating COBC reports, KBR filed an "emergency" motion with the U.S. Court of Appeals for the District of Columbia Circuit, seeking interlocutory review of the lower court's order. KBR claimed that the judge had overstepped well-established legal boundaries by ordering the release of the COBC reports, and specifically claimed that the court's order would set precedent that internal investigations conducted pursuant to mandatory government regulations could not be kept confidential under the attorney-client privilege.

Shortly thereafter business associations aligned with KBR, including the Chamber of Commerce, the National Association of Manufacturers and the Association of Corporate Counsel, submitted an *amicus curie* "friend of the court" brief to the appeals court in support of KBR. These groups warned that any undermining of the ability of corporate General Counsel to keep documents confidential would have a catastrophic impact on the willingness of companies to engage in effective internal compliance activities.

The old legal axiom applies to the Barko case—bad facts make bad law. And the facts for KBR are very bad. KBR failed to take the steps, known to any first year law student, to preserve the attorney-client privilege. KBR's use of a non-disclosure agreement, as opposed to basic *Upjohn* protections, clearly raised significant issues suggesting that KBR was more interested in preventing disclosure of the facts without seeking to protect the internal investigation by following basic attorney-client privilege procedures.

KBR's sloppy post hoc attempt to rescue the attorney-client privilege claim ignores the overwhelming factual problems with KBR's handling of the internal investigation.[20]

At the time of this article, the Court of Appeals has not decided the *Barko* case. As explained, the Court of Appeals will have a hard time finding that KBR followed any proper procedures in conducting the internal investigation. The mere fact that the results of the investigation were reported to KBR's general counsel is not sufficient, by itself, to uphold the privilege. Such a holding would be contrary to the requirements set forth by the Supreme Court in *Upjohn* and cases decided following *Upjohn*. Whether the trial judge's rationale is upheld will be a closer question since the Court of Appeals may find its own reasoning for rejecting KBR's privilege claims.

The Federal Rules of Civil Procedure "strongly favor full discovery whenever possible."[21] "The purpose of the attorney-client privilege is to encourage open and complete communication

---

[20] Regardless of the outcome of the appeal, one fact in the case will be hotly contested for some time to come: the legality of the non-disclosure agreement KBR required its employees to sign whenever they provided witness statements under its COBC program. This non-disclosure agreement, which was heavily relied upon by the district court in ruling that the COBC investigatory reports were not privileged, placed strict prohibitions on employees. Employees were threatened with discharge if they discussed their fraud allegations with anyone, and were told that disclosures of their concerns could harm KBR's business in the Middle East.

[21] Farnsworth v. Proctor & Gamble Co., 758 F.2d 1545, 1547 (11th Cir. 1985).21 501 F. Supp. 2d 789, 795 (E.D. La. 2007); see FED. R. CIV. P. 26(b)(5).

between a client and his attorney by eliminating the possibility of subsequent compelled disclosure of their confidential communications."[22]

For the privilege to apply, a party invoking the attorney-client privilege must show "(1) a communication between client and counsel that (2) was intended to be and was in fact kept confidential, and (3) was made for the purpose of obtaining or providing legal advice."[23]

"[T]he attorney-client privilege applies to corporations" and protects communications to corporate counsel for purpose of obtaining legal advice.[24] Communications between corporate client and corporate counsel require the proponent to satisfy a "purpose and intent" threshold test. "[M]odern corporate counsel have become involved in all facets of the enterprises for which they work. As a consequence, in-house legal counsel participates in and renders decisions about business, technical, scientific, public relations, and advertising issues, as well as purely legal issues."[25]

The privilege also protects "communications between corporate employees in which prior [legal] advice received is being transmitted to those who have a need to know in the scope of their corporate responsibilities."[26] In some cases, the privilege may also be extended to protect "information gathered by corporate employees for transmission to corporate counsel for the rendering of legal advice[.]"[27]

Under controlling law, if the "primary purpose" of the COBC investigation was to obtain legal advice, the documents could potentially be shielded from review. However, if the "primary

---

[22] See In re Colton, 201 F. Supp. 13, 15 (S.D.N.Y. 1961), affd, 306 F.2d 633 (2d Cir.1962), cert. denied, 371 U.S. 951 (1963) (basis of the privilege is "to encourage clients to make the fullest disclosures to their attorneys, to enable the latter properly to advise the clients"); United States v. United Shoe Mach. Corp., 89 F. *Supp.* 357, 358 (D. Mass. 1950) ("To induce clients to make [free and honest] communications, the privilege to prevent their later disclosure is said by courts and commentators to be a necessity.") (emphasis added); In re Seroquel Prod. Liab. Litig., No. 6:06-md-1769-Orl-22DAB, 2008 WL 1995058, at *2 (M.D. Fla. May 7, 2008) (citing United States v. Noriega, 917 F.2d 1543, 1550 [11th Cir. 1990]). The privilege applies only to communications and does not extend to facts. *See* Upjohn Co. v. United States, 449 U.S. at 395–96.

[23] In re Teleglobe Comm. Corp., 493 F.3d 345, 359 (3d Cir. 2007); In re County of Erie, 473 F.3d 413, 419 (2d Cir. 2007); United States v. Noriega, 917 F.2d 1543, 1550 (11th Cir. 1990).

[24] Upjohn Co. v. United States, supra, 449 U.S. at 390. The Court stressed that the privilege allowed corporate counsel to have all the relevant information "to enable him to give sound and informed advice." Id. at 390.

[25] In re Vioxx Prods. Liab. Litig., 501 F. Supp. 2d 789, 797 (E.D. La. 2007). Simply labeling a document "Confidential—Attorney Client Privilege" is not an adequate basis for legally presuming or even logically assuming a primary legal purpose. In re Vioxx, 501 F. Supp. 2d at 797. "The content of the message must request legal assistance, and the information conveyed must be reasonably related to the assistance sought." Rice, Electronic Evidence 260; Tyne v. Time Warner Entm't Co., 212 F.R.D. 596 n.4 (M.D. Fla. 2002) (the attorney-client privilege "label may serve to put recipients on notice that the document is confidential, but it does not at all prove the existence of privilege.").

[26] In re Vioxx, 501 F. Supp. 2d at 797.

[27] 1 Edna Selan Epstein, The Attorney-Client Privilege and the Work Product Doctrine 151-52 (5th ed. 2007) (The court, relying on the proposed but never adopted Rule 503(b) of the federal rules, "concluded it was not necessary for the attorney to be either the sender or direct recipient of the privileged communications. The documents at issue were documents gathered to prepare a patent application and forward to patent counsel.") (citing In Eutectic v. Metco, 61 F.R.D. 35, 37 [E.D.N.Y 1973]).

purpose" of the investigation was business related, the mere fact that attorneys reviewed the documents or had supervisory responsibilities over the COBC program would not, onto itself, shield the documents from discovery. Unfortunately for KBR, the COBC investigation was conducted without any adherence to the basic procedural requirements dictated by the Supreme Court under *Upjohn* and long-standing precedent.[28]

To deflect attention from KBR's own procedural missteps and mishandling of the COBC internal investigation, KBR is arguing, with the support of powerful business interests, that upholding the trial judge's decision would undermine the ability of companies to conduct internal investigations under the protection of the attorney-client privilege.

KBR's argument assumes too much, and ignores the fact that its own procedural missteps have placed it in a situation where they have nothing left to argue but dramatic distractions from basic legal principles. KBR's attempt to expand the "privilege" and keep clearly discoverable information away from the regulators and the public would be contrary to the public interest and to the purposes of the attorney-client privilege itself.

Moreover, KBR's argument would set a dangerous precedent by suggesting that companies will need to conduct more of their compliance operations under the umbrella of privilege. Such a result would run contrary to the important need of compliance programs to be transparent within a company's culture. A compliance program managed purely as an arm of the legal function runs the serious risk of being perceived as, and in fact of becoming, less a means of preventing and detecting misconduct, and instead more of an information-gathering exercise for giving legal advice.[29]

KBR's argument, carried to its logical extreme, would encourage companies to place more of their compliance operations under an umbrella of privilege by returning compliance officers to a place they do not belong—reporting to the General Counsel. This would be an enormous backward step in the development of effective compliance programs, and would have the unfortunate result of increasing privilege claims over routine compliance operations.

KBR maintains that the integrity of corporate compliance programs is threatened by the lower court's disclosure order. However, it is KBR's failure to follow basic procedures that, in the end, has forced KBR to make a dramatic and flawed argument: namely, that the lower court's decision will have disastrous impact on the future ability of corporations to conduct internal investigations under the attorney-client privilege.

---

[28] The COBC investigative forms included no references to the fact that the KBR investigators were reporting to General Counsel, and nowhere on the form were employees informed that the information they were providing would be classified by the company as "attorney client privileged." Order at 5-6.

[29] *See* http://www.corpcounsel.com/id=1202649856926/GM-InHouse-Lawyers-Pulled-Into-Ignition-Switch-Probe?slreturn=20140711121020

IV. The Way Forward for General Counsels and Chief Compliance Officers

Every company needs the attorney-client privilege to promote internal communications on legal issues to ensure legal compliance. Such communications are critical to the General Counsel's ability to promote and ensure a company's compliance with the law.

CCOs carry out their compliance activities with a presumption of transparency and disclosure. After all, the success of a compliance program depends on its visibility within an organization as one important means to communicate and create a culture of integrity. At the same time, a significant benefit of an effective compliance program is being able to share it proactively with regulators and prosecutors when it matters. "Sorry our compliance program is privileged" doesn't quite cut it. Most of the compliance functions are carried out with this transparency in mind. And, then there is the other legal axiom well known to GCs: "when everything is privileged, nothing is privileged." This is a warning to those who would argue for a blanket privilege for any part of a compliance program simply due to the fact that it reports to the legal department.

However, when appropriate, strict protection of the company's attorney-client and work product privileges can be asserted by timely involvement of in-house or outside counsel. As suggested in a widely circulated Ethisphere white paper, "The Business Case for a Standalone Chief Compliance Officer":

> Effective programs are thoroughly documented, as are related investigations. Such documentation not only reflects the components of the program in the event of an investigation, but also demonstrates that the company is responding to issues that are reported or discovered by refashioning its internal controls.[30]

So how exactly should legal privilege be addressed in an effective compliance program that is independent from the legal function?

CCOs understand that an important corporate partner is the General Counsel.[31] The ultimate success of a compliance program often depends on this relationship—if they do not get along, the compliance function may be compromised. CCOs and General Counsels need each other and need to recognize this fact. When they do, they can build effective programs to work together when conducting risk assessments, internal investigations, compliance program assessments and evaluations and other sensitive compliance functions. But none of this cooperation and collaboration requires that the CCO report to, or be filtered by, the General Counsel. In fact, a relationship where one party can automatically veto the mandate and judgment of the other party

---

[30] The Business Case for a Standalone Chief Compliance Officer, available at https://ethisphere.site-ym.com/store/ViewProduct.aspx?id=621756 (visited June 10, 2014).

[31] CCOs in the SCCE survey view Legal as close and valued allies with whom they enjoy a positive working relationship; cited in this Corporate Counsel column: http://compliancestrategists.com/csblog/wp-content/uploads/2013/11/Making-the-CCO-an-Independent-Voice-in-the-C-Suite.pdf

has the opposite effect from collaboration, and deprives the company of an important, independent voice in the C-Suite.[32]

Any compliance project that requires preservation of the privilege can be conducted in a manner that protects the confidentiality and corporate privilege. For instance, the cloak of legal privilege is critical in those instances when the company needs actual legal advice, such as when an opinion is necessary to determine whether a company has actually violated the law and advice is needed to help remediate the violation and improve compliance functions. This process requires the participation of in-house or outside counsel. The CCO depends on the legal department in these situations, and should be fully sensitive to the significance of the privilege.

The coordination function is equally important when it comes to responding to a whistleblower complaint and the risk that the whistleblower will report the matter to the federal or state government. The CCO and the General Counsel should work hand-in-hand to address the whistleblower complaint, interact with the whistleblower, and provide assurances to the whistleblower of the company's intention to investigate and remediate any problems that they discover—a required practice under the amendments to the Sentencing Guidelines.

Any suggestion that CCOs need to continue reporting to the corporate legal department to protect the privilege is not only incorrect, as noted in the Ethisphere white paper, it is "contrary to the goals of an effective compliance and ethics program."[33]

Moreover, it ignores the overwhelming governance trend and the accomplishments of many CCOs and General Counsels who have worked together successfully to carry out their respective responsibilities. Separation of the legal and compliance functions ensures independent and objective legal reviews, and promotes an internal system of checks and balances. What is critical is that the two roles coordinate and work well together by establishing some basic "interface" ground rules and ensuring that their respective mandates are clear, documented, understood by all relevant personnel, and implemented. As many commentators have observed, the two roles are unique, with separate mandates and required competencies, and are ideally carried out by two different people.

In this new and challenging ethics and compliance environment, General Counsels and CCOs need to coordinate and develop specific protocols for identifying potentially significant issues, protecting the company's ability to rely on the privilege, and implementing policies and procedures to ensure that the privilege is maintained, or to review the continuing applicability of the privilege to the specific issue on an ongoing basis. The new protocol for coordination of legal and compliance functions should not be very hard to define but will depend on good faith by the parties to adhere to the standards, communicate with each other as needed, and not use the

[32] Donna Boehme, Making the CCO an Independent Voice in the C-Suite, Corporate Counsel, http://compliancestrategists.com/csblog/wp-content/uploads/2013/11/Making-the-CCO-an-Independent-Voice-in-the-C-Suite.pdf

[33] *Id.* at 8.

protocol as a means to manipulate or skew internal politics to either side's benefit. It is a challenge for legal and compliance professionals to work together.

When it comes to internal investigations, with certain exceptions, it is fairly easy to identify those investigations that will require the protection of the privilege. The exceptional cases will require a conservative approach—meaning use of the privilege unless and until a determination is made that the privilege is no longer necessary. Whatever rules are applied, the parties have to ensure consistency and be willing to make adjustments as needed.

The way forward for General Counsels and CCOs requires a distancing from the past—the issue of reporting relationships, supremacy and control are gone. The new era of cooperation is beginning. Let us all hope that like the ending line of *Casablanca*, the new relationship between the General Counsel and the CCO is "the beginning of a beautiful friendship."

Learning the Hard Way: Ethics and Compliance Program Lessons Gleaned from Recent U.S. Resolution Agreements

Peter Jaffe, Chief Ethics and Compliance Officer, The AES Corporation
Michael Diamant, Partner Gibson, Dunn & Crutcher LLP

A little more than a decade ago, few public companies outside of the financial and healthcare sectors had a dedicated, internal compliance function. Today, a dedicated compliance function has become the norm, and Compliance and Ethics ("C&E") programs have correspondingly gained in significance, resourcing, and visibility. Historically, compliance officers were rarely a part of senior management or the C-suite. Today, by contrast, compliance officers have become increasingly elevated and independent within management, and increasingly pivotal in their contributions to the day-to-day operation of major companies.

The federal government has been a key driver in this evolution, first through the Federal Sentencing Guidelines for Organizations, and more recently through consent orders, deferred prosecution agreements, and other resolution agreements connected to the investigation of suspected corporate wrongdoing. Increasingly, federal authorities have included detailed requirements for a corporate defendant's compliance program as part of the injunctive relief included in a resolution agreement. Thus, resolution agreements, and the obligations contained within them, have become more and more important as a source of guidance and prescriptive authority. Resolutions can provide insight into the government's view of the elements of an effective compliance program and how such programs should be implemented. In turn, that insight can be more broadly instructive to corporations in designing, staffing, and implementing their own compliance programs. In point of fact, that insight has already begun to "spill over," with some organizations outside the resolution arena voluntarily adopting related compliance reforms as a leading indicator of good practice.

In this paper, we identify some key lessons contained in recent U.S. Department of Justice ("DOJ") and U.S. Securities and Exchange Commission ("SEC") corporate non-prosecution and deferred prosecution agreements, as well as U.S. Department of Health and Human Services ("HHS") corporate integrity agreements. We bring to this discussion our respective experiences as an in-house compliance counsel at a major public company and as an external advisor to many such companies.

Lessons from Recent Resolutions

Deferred prosecution agreements and other resolution agreements reflect a trend toward increasing government interest in compliance programs as a basic remedial measure to resolve criminal and civil investigations. As early as 2007, DOJ included specific requirements for compliance programs in some of its resolutions, but the number of elements typically included was only nine. More recent resolution agreements have included as many as 18 explicit compliance program elements.[1] Many of the elements commonly included in DOJ resolutions are based on the Federal Sentencing Guidelines and the Guidelines' blueprint for what constitutes an effective compliance program. Even so, DOJ resolution agreements provide additional color on those elements and on how DOJ views and interprets the elements of effective compliance. More recent DOJ resolutions have gone even further, with mandates for a range of deeper implementation practices in compliance, touching on the strength of corporate culture; the oversight role of the Board or committees of the Board; the authority, positioning and independence of the Chief Compliance Officer ("CCO"); and the role of management in supporting compliance.

Requirements for effective compliance programs gleaned from recent DOJ resolution agreements include the following:

- *High-Level Commitment*: Strong, explicit, and visible support from senior management and directors.
- *Policies and Procedures*: A written compliance code including appropriate policies and procedures addressing, *inter alia*, gifts, hospitality, entertainment, customer travel, political contributions, charitable donations and sponsorships, facilitation payments, solicitation, and extortion, as well as a reasonably designed financial controls system.
- *Periodic Risk-Based Review*: Risk-based development of the aforementioned policies and procedures, as well as at least annual review and update of these policies and procedures to take into account evolving international and industry standards.
- *Proper Oversight and Independence*: One or more senior executives charged with implementation and oversight of compliance responsibilities who report or have the authority to report to independent bodies, including internal audit, the board, and/or a board committee.
- *Training and Guidance*: Effective communication of the compliance code, policies, and procedures throughout the company and its business partners; periodic training on these policies; and annual certifications of compliance with training requirements. In addition, a mechanism to provide guidance and advice on complying with the code, policies, or procedures.
- *Internal Reporting and Investigation*: A system for internal, confidential reporting of policy violations, as well as an effective system for investigating these reports.
- *Enforcement and Discipline*: Mechanisms to enforce the compliance program and appropriate disciplinary procedures.

---

[1] Compare Paradigm B.V. NPA, App'x B (Sept. 21, 2007) with Parker Drilling Co. DPA, Attach. C (Apr. 15, 2013). Note that while the corporate compliance program elements are most often designated Attachment C, sometimes these elements may be Attachments B or D, depending on the number and type of various certifications attached to the end of deferred prosecution agreements. See, e.g., Archer Daniels Midland Co. DPA, Attach. B (Dec. 20, 2013); Hewlett-Packard Polska, SP. Z O.O. DPA, Attach. D (Apr. 9, 2014). Note that Professors Brandon Garrett and Jon Ashley of the University of Virginia maintain a database of all publically available DPAs here: http://lib.law.virginia.edu/Garrett/prosecution_agreements/DP (visited June 10, 2014).

- *Third-Party Relationships*: Risk-based due diligence program pertaining to agents, business partners, or other third-parties and appropriate contractual guarantees that third-parties will comply with anti-corruption laws.
- *Mergers and Acquisitions*: Risk-based due diligence program for mergers and acquisition activity, including the prompt integration of the newly acquired entity into the company's compliance program.
- *Monitoring and Testing*: Periodic testing and review of the compliance code, policies, and procedures and taking into account relevant developments and evolving international and industry standards.

Looking across these thematic elements from recent resolution agreements, we would like to offer several broad observations and suggestions about the implications for compliance. It is important to keep in mind that these obligations are part of resolutions of enforcement actions and are imposed on companies alleged to have gone astray. All of these elements may not be required for every company, in every industry, of all sizes and levels of sophistication. But for companies seeking to respond proactively to DOJ, the SEC, and their sister agencies, the trends in recent resolution agreements offers important insight into how expectations for compliance programs may evolve in the future.

1. Recent Resolution Agreements Increasingly Emphasize Risk-Based Approaches to Compliance, but Raise Continuing Questions for Companies and Their Compliance Officers

As the recent joint DOJ-SEC Resource Guide to the Foreign Corrupt Practices Act ("FCPA")[2] emphasizes, many of the requirements contained in resolution agreements emphasize the importance of a risk-based approach to compliance. A thoughtful, analytical approach to identifying, measuring, and addressing key compliance risks is critical to an effective C&E program, as is the application of risk-based compliance logic to policies and procedures, periodic reviews, training, third-party relationships, and mergers and acquisitions. Many questions remain, however, regarding what a "risk based approach" to all of these aspects of compliance fully entails. Is there one standard that defines appropriate risk tolerance across all companies and all situations, or is it up to every individual company to define the level of risk it reasonably deems appropriate for its situation? Is it appropriate for company management to weigh compliance risks against available compliance resources? Will the government use evidence of a compliance violation alone to argue that a company did not appropriately identify and address its underlying compliance risks?

Absent answers to these sorts of questions, what we can conclude is that the federal government is recognizing the importance of a well-thought-out risk-based approach to compliance in the context of government resolution and enforcement activity. Companies will

---

[2] DOJ & SEC (2012), FCPA: A Resource Guide to the U.S. Foreign Corrupt Practices Act. Available for download at http://www.justice.gov/criminal/fraud/fcpa/guide.pdf (visited June 10, 2014).

need to wrestle with deep questions about how to design and implement an approach to compliance risks, in order to fulfill a standard that is continuing to emerge through government resolution agreements.

2. More Compliance Obligations Are Being Imposed on Boards and Managers Through Government Resolution Agreements

Some recent resolution agreements specify board-level oversight of the compliance program, with additional related requirements for boards such as annual compliance certifications or board-level compliance training. DOJ resolutions commonly require that the chief compliance officer ("CCO") be given unfiltered access to communicate with the Board or with a committee of the Board, and some resolutions further require that directors provide strong, explicit, and visible support for the compliance program.[3] Similarly, HHS corporate integrity agreements now contain standard provisions imposing board compliance oversight responsibilities.

For example, the behemoth 101-page Johnson & Johnson corporate integrity agreement (signed in October 2013) includes a long list of compliance program requirements, not least being three-year executive compensation clawbacks, board-level compliance training, and compliance certifications both for the board and for designated persons in management.[4] Similar mandates for compliance certification have, in particular, been included in several other recent HHS corporate integrity agreements. Notably, these mandates tend to be particularly detailed, requiring certifications from business unit heads, as well as vice presidents in charge of human resources, strategy, medical affairs, communication, finance, and chief scientific officers.[5] As a policy matter, this requirement is reminiscent of the CEO and CFO internal controls certifications required under the Sarbanes-Oxley Act, although the requirements for compliance certification permeate much further down the corporate chain of command.[6] To our knowledge, the HHS practice of mandating compliance certifications has not so far spread to DOJ or SEC corporate resolutions, but it could do so in the future.

The take-away here is that resolution agreements increasingly spotlight boards and senior managers as having specific compliance obligations, moving somewhat beyond the contours of the Federal Sentencing Guidelines. Not only have resolution agreements compelled boards and managers to undertake more compliance training and more compliance oversight, but directors and management have also been required to take on more direct and explicit responsibility through certification mandates (at least on the HHS side). At least in companies involved in

---

[3] See Archer Daniels Midland Co. Non-Prosecution Agreement ("NPA"), Attach. B, 1, 7 (Dec. 20, 2013).

[4] Corporate Integrity Agreement between the Office of Inspector Gen. of the Dep't of Health & Human Servs. and Johnson & Johnson, at 8–10, 24, 32 (Oct. 13, 2013) ("J&J CIA"); see also Corporate Integrity Agreement between the Office of Inspector Gen. of the Dep't of Health & Human Servs. and GlaxoSmithKline LLC (June 28, 2012).

[5] Id.; see also HHS CIAs with Bayer Healthcare LLC (Nov. 25, 2008); Eli Lilly and Co. (Jan. 14, 2009); AstraZeneca LP (Apr. 27, 2010); Allergan (Aug. 30, 2012); Abbott Pharmaceuticals (May 7, 2012).

[6] Sarbanes Oxley Act, Pub. L. No. 107-204, §§ 302, 906, 116 Stat. 745, 777–78, 806 (July 20, 2002).

regulatory resolutions, if this trend continues there is likely to be increasing pressure on boards and management to become knowledgeable about their companies' compliance activities and to play an active role in compliance endeavors in the future.

3. Government Resolutions Are Placing More Compliance Emphasis on Due Diligence and Management of Third Parties

Several recent resolutions involve allegations of corporate misconduct through third-party intermediaries, underscoring the importance of effective compliance due diligence programs to vet business partners. This area plays a particularly central role in compliance with the FCPA, in light of the statute's aggressive attenuated liability standards. The December 20, 2013, Archer Daniels Midland ("ADM") FCPA resolution is a good illustration.[7] There, according to the criminal information, ADM's German and Ukrainian subsidiaries engaged third-party intermediaries in a scheme to kick-back 18 to 20% of the value of VAT refunds to Ukrainian tax officials in return for the officials releasing the refunds due to ADM. In total, between 2002 and 2008, the ADM subsidiaries are alleged to have paid $22 million to secure the release of more than $100 million in VAT refunds. In brief, the ADM resolution agreement compelled the company to tighten its compliance controls and due diligence in connection with the actions of its subsidiaries and intermediaries going forward.

Due diligence on third-party intermediaries is also becoming a focal point in resolution agreements outside of the anti-corruption space. For example, the Johnson & Johnson corporate integrity agreement required J&J to undertake numerous obligations related to third-party personnel by imposing downstream compliance obligations and controls in the context of its various third-party relationships.[8]

In a companion white paper in this volume, Scott Killingsworth[9] writes in detail about emerging trends in "private" compliance, as companies impose increasing compliance burdens on each other through a web of bilateral contracts. Federal government enforcement activity and resolutions are amplifying the same trend by creating explicit requirements for more third-party due diligence. In resolution agreements, the government is increasingly focusing on third-party due diligence processes and procedures, and on the actions companies involved in resolutions are taking to monitor the actions of commercial partners and counterparties. Once again, the expectation is that CCOs will take a risk-based approach to identifying and mitigating this risk.

---

[7] Press Release, Dep't of Justice, ADM Subsidiary Pleads Guilty to Conspiracy to Violate the Foreign Corrupt Practices Act (Dec. 20, 2013), available at http://www.justice.gov/opa/pr/2013/December/13-crm-1356.html (June 10, 2014).

[8] J&J CIA, at 11, 36.

[9] *See* Scott Killingsworth, The Privatization of Compliance (2014), this volume.

4. Recent Enforcement Activity Spotlights the Importance of Compliance Training and Management Engagement as Mitigating Factors

Recent resolutions suggest that robust employee training and communication on compliance issues are key elements to an effective compliance program that may, in some circumstances, even help a company avoid corporate penalties for the actions of a rogue employee. For example, in April 2012, a former Morgan Stanley executive, Garth Peterson, pleaded guilty to charges for conspiring to evade Morgan Stanley's internal accounting controls. Mr. Peterson had, among other indiscretions, surreptitiously transferred an ownership interest in one of Shanghai's buildings from a Morgan Stanley fund to himself and his friend, who was a Chinese government official. DOJ declined to prosecute Morgan Stanley, citing its internal controls, regularly updated compliance policies, and extensive compliance training program.[10] Above and beyond Morgan Stanley's ongoing compliance program monitoring, random audits, due diligence on all new business partners, and controls on payments, the extensive training program cited included well-documented anti-corruption training directed to Morgan Stanley's Asia employees on 54 occasions during the relevant period, FCPA training for Mr. Peterson on at least seven occasions, and FCPA compliance reminders to Mr. Peterson at least 35 occasions.[11]

The Morgan Stanley case demonstrates the importance of compliance training in DOJ's analysis of the culpability of an organization for the actions of a rogue employee, especially when the rogue employee evades the requirements of a robust compliance program, flouting clear compliance directives from management. In consequence, companies and their CCOs would be well advised to consider robust and documented compliance training activities as an important component to mitigating the risk of material violations perpetrated by rogue actors who intentionally violate the law.

5. Compliance Risk through Marketing Activities Is Another Focal Point in Recent Resolution Agreements

Recent resolutions and enforcement activity suggest that CCOs should continue to concentrate on the corporate marketing and sales function, and focus compliance training efforts in this area. Related risk has been increasingly important in the healthcare compliance area, with the dramatic

---

[10] Press Release, U.S. Securities and Exchange Commission, SEC Charges Former Morgan Stanley Executive with FCPA Violations and Investment Adviser Fraud (April 25, 2012), available at https://www.sec.gov/News/PressRelease/Detail/PressRelease/1365171488702#.U3Yn2Ch8qko (visited June 10, 2014).

[11] *See* discussion in Davis Polk, Morgan Stanley's FCPA Declination and the Benefits of Effective Compliance, October 9, 2012, available at http://www.davispolk.com/files/uploads/Webcasts//Morgan.Stanley.FCPA.Webinar.FINAL.2012.10.02.pdf (visited June 10, 2014).

increase in pharmaceutical off-label marketing cases over the past decade.[12] But the concern over the marketing and sales function cuts across industries, and examples of related compliance failures are not limited to those involving a vast international FCPA conspiracy or a multibillion dollar pharmaceutical case. For example, on August 30, 2013, Bashas' Inc., a family-owned grocery store chain, entered into a non-prosecution agreement with DOJ, after an investigation revealed "Prime" tenderloins being sold at certain Bashas'-owned AJ's stores in Arizona that were actually lesser-quality "Choice" tenderloins, as well as the sale of mislabeled "Kobe" beef cuts.[13] DOJ agreed that senior management had no knowledge of this practice, but nevertheless faulted the company for an administrative consolidation at in the corporate meat department that "fail[ed] to provide adequate corporate oversight over the operations of individual AJ's locations."[14]

The lesson from the resolution in *Bashas'* is that in some cases DOJ expects corporate compliance efforts to penetrate all the way to the individual store meat-counter level. The failure to do so cost Bashas' nearly $1.5 million in restitution, in addition to other fees, costs, and reputational harm. By extension, where a company is involved in local-level retail sales and marketing, its compliance function may need to drill down to the local level in its monitoring and training efforts.

6. Recent Resolution Agreements Focus on the Roles and Responsibilities of the CCO and the CCO's Ability to Communicate Directly with the Board or a Board Committee

Recent criminal and civil resolution resolutions have provided new insight into regulators' views on the authority and independence of the CCO, both as formalized in the management structure of an organization and as implemented through channels of communication to independent authorities, such as the board of directors and internal audit.

In 1998, the HHS Office of Inspector General cautioned against having CCOs report to the General Counsel or CFO.[15] Subsequent HHS corporate integrity agreements went further, requiring that the CCO be a member of "senior management," and precluding the CCO from reporting to or serving as the General Counsel or CFO.[16] In 2008, HHS extended this trend and began explicitly requiring a direct reporting relationship to the CEO—a requirement that

---

[12] *See* David W. Bradford, John L. Turner, & Jonathan W. Williams, Off-Label Use of Pharmaceuticals: Trends and Drivers, at 1, April 22, 2013. Available at http://papers.ssrn.com/sol3/papers.cfm?abstract_id=2230976 (visited June 10, 2014).

[13] Bashas' Inc. NPA, at 1.

[14] Id. at ¶ 4.

[15] Office of Inspector General, Dep't of Health & Human Servs., Compliance Program Guidance for Hospitals, 63 Fed. Reg. 8987, 8993 n.35 (Feb. 23, 1998).

[16] *See*, e.g., Corporate Integrity Agreement between the Office of Inspector Gen. of the Dep't of Health & Human Servs. and Serono Holding, Inc., at 5–6 (Oct. 14, 2005); Corporate Integrity Agreement between the Office of Inspector Gen. of the Dep't of Health & Human Servs. and Boston Scientific Corp., at 5 (Dec. 23, 2009).

continues to this day.[17] For example, on February 21, 2014, Endo Health Solutions Inc. and its subsidiary Endo Pharmaceuticals paid $192.7 million to resolve DOJ and HHS criminal and civil regulatory actions arising from of the marketing of off-label uses for the prescription anesthetic Lidoderm.[18] Both Endo's deferred prosecution agreement with DOJ and its corporate integrity agreement with HHS require that Endo's CCO report to its CEO. Both agreements also require that Endo's CCO make regular compliance reports to Endo's board of directors. This reporting structure is most frequently imposed by HHS resolution agreements in the context of healthcare cases. DOJ and the SEC tend recognize a wider variety of reporting structures and are less likely to preclude the unity of the legal and compliance functions.

While many companies' CCOs report to their general counsels—and do so for well-thought purposes in an effort to have the most effective compliance programs within their organizational structure and operating environment—other companies, particularly in the healthcare and financial services sectors, appear to be following the government's lead by having the CCO report to the Board, a committee of the Board, or the CEO. For example, a number of large banks have split their compliance departments from their legal departments, including giants such as Barclays and JPMorgan.[19] The HSBC deferred prosecution agreement even took the unusual step of requiring that the CCO be elevated to the ranks of the top 50 managers of the firm.[20] Of course, in some contexts, depending on many factors, including the nature of the business, the size and sophistication of the company, and the compliance risks it faces, among others, a company may reasonably determine that it would be more effective in its situation to unite the compliance and legal departments.

Without addressing the long-running argument over the structural pros and cons of having the CCO report directly to the CEO, we instead spotlight a more basic point regarding government enforcement efforts: namely, that resolution agreements have increasingly focused on the positioning of the CCO within the organization, and on ensuring the CCO has unfettered communication access to both senior executives and the Board. Even when they do not segregate the CCO to an independent function, several recent DOJ non-prosecution and deferred prosecution agreements have focused on ensuring an open line of communication between the

---

[17] *See*, e.g., Corporate Integrity Agreement between the Office of Inspector Gen. of the Dep't of Health & Human Servs. and The Jackson-Madison Cnty. Gen. Hosp. Dist., at 2 (Nov. 26, 2008); Corporate Integrity Agreement between the Office of Inspector Gen. of the Dep't of Health & Human Servs. and Pacific Health Corp., et al., at 4 (Jun. 8, 2012).

[18] Press Release, Dep't of Justice, Endo Pharmaceuticals and Endo Health Solutions to Pay $192.7 Million to Resolve Criminal and Civil Liability Relating to Marketing of Prescription Drug Lidoderm for Unapproved Uses (Feb. 21, 2014), available at http://www.justice.gov/opa/pr/2014/February/14-civ-187.html (last visited May 13, 2014).

[19] Bora Yagiz, Better Career Paths, New Reporting Lines as Compliance Gains Status at Banks, Reuters Financial Regulatory Reform, Mar. 20, 2014. Available at http://blogs.reuters.com/financial-regulatory-forum/2014/03/20/better-career-paths-new-reporting-lines-as-compliance-gains-status-at-banks-global-report/ (visited June 10, 2014).

[20] *See* HSBC Bank USA, N.A. and HSBC Holdings PLC DPA, ¶ 5 (Dec. 11, 2012).

CCO and senior oversight authorities within the company, notably including boards. For example, the previously mentioned ADM non-prosecution agreement contained language requiring that the CCO "have the *authority to report directly* to independent monitoring bodies," such as internal audit and the board.[21] In addition, the ADM resolution agreement, like some others, contains requirements that the CCO have an "adequate level of autonomy from management," and that the CCO be provided "sufficient resources . . . to maintain [his or her] autonomy."[22]

At least four other deferred and non-prosecution agreements reached in 2013 by DOJ and the SEC have explicitly required the company's CCO have "direct reporting obligations to independent monitoring bodies, including internal audit, the Company's board of directors," or an appropriate board committee.[23] The general movement of recent resolution agreements in this direction notably follows the logic of the joint DOJ-SEC Resource Guide on the FCPA,[24] as well as the logic of the Federal Sentencing Guidelines,[25] both of which underline the need for a reporting channel between the CCO and the "governing authority" of a corporation (i.e., the Board), in order to safeguard the autonomy of the CCO and the effectiveness of the compliance program that he or she operates.

For companies, the most practical take-away from all of this is that resolution agreements have placed increasing emphasis on the role of the CCO, the CCO's reporting relationships appropriate to its industry and operations, and the authority and communication channels of the CCO. In addition, ensuring the CCO has the appropriate empowerment also allows governing boards to be able to carry out their own compliance oversight responsibility. Recent resolutions have included a range of specific provisions and requirements along these lines. Broadly, these agreements are increasingly focusing on the CCOs' empowerment, as well as effective and open lines of communication to directors, senior managers, and others to ensure that unfiltered CCO communications can reach the senior governing authorities of the corporation.

Conclusion

In recent years, DOJ, HHS, and other regulators have become increasingly focused on corporate ethics and compliance programs, their structure, their implementation, and their power to address

---

[21] Archer Daniels Midland Co. NPA, Attach. B, ¶ 7 (emphasis added); *see also* Weatherford Int'l DPA, Attach. C, ¶ 7 (Nov. 26, 2013); Bilfinger SE DPA, Attach. C, ¶ 7 (Dec. 9, 2013).

[22] Archer Daniels Midland Co. NPA, Attach. B., ¶ 7.

[23] Ralph Lauren Corp. NPA, Attach. C, ¶ 7 (Apr. 22, 2013); Total, S.A. DPA, Attach C, ¶ 6 (May 23, 2013); Diebold, Inc. DPA, Attach. C, ¶ 7 (Oct. 15, 2013); ArthroCare DPA, Attach. C. ¶ 7 (Dec. 30, 2013). See also Las Vegas Sands Corp. NPA, Attach. B, ¶ 1 (Aug. 26, 2013) (requiring an overall compliance structure with "oversight by an independent Committee of the Board of Directors with direct oversight of the Company's Chief Compliance Officer [] and the Compliance Program.").

[24] *See* U.S. Dep't of Justice and U.S. Securities & Exch. Comm'n, A Resource Guide to the U.S. Foreign Corrupt Practices Act 58 (Nov. 12, 2012).

[25] U.S. Sentencing Guidelines § 8B2.1(2)(C) (2013).

risks and prevent violations of law and regulation. The government's focus has notably manifested itself through resolution agreements, which discharge civil and criminal investigations and prosecutions against corporate wrongdoers. Such resolution agreements can exert influence on the business community, not only through their direct impact on the defendants who specifically enter into them but also, more broadly, as sources of guidance on compliance best practice. They illustrate what enforcement agencies are looking for when they review the vitality and effectiveness of a compliance program. Trends toward more explicit risk-based approaches to compliance, a greater emphasis on third-party due diligence, open and direct lines of communication, and effective training programs that permeate an organization all serve to underscore a more basic point. Namely, federal corporate resolution agreements are increasingly focusing on the effectiveness of compliance programs as remedial measures, often setting forth detailed requirements for an effective compliance program in the context of each case. This shows an increasing interest among regulators about the role an effective compliance program can play in preventing future violations. Companies can learn from these agreements and evaluate whether the provisions set forth in them are right for them.

References

Castillo, Ruben, "The Technology Challenge of the United States' Aggressive Compliance Environment," in Michael D. Greenberg, *Culture, Compliance, and the C-Suite: How Executives, Boards, and Policymakers Can Better Safeguard Against Misconduct at the Top*, pp. 33–38, Santa Monica, Calif.: RAND Corporation, CF-316-CCEG, 2013.

Greenberg, Michael D., *Perspectives of Chief Ethics and Compliance Officers on the Detection and Prevention of Corporate Misdeeds: What the Policy Community Should Know*, Santa Monica, Calif.: RAND Corporation, CF-258-RC, 2009. As of August 18, 2014: http://www.rand.org/pubs/conf_proceedings/CF258.html

———, *Directors as Guardians of Compliance and Ethics Within the Corporate Citadel: What the Policy Community Should Know*, Santa Monica, Calif.: RAND Corporation, CF-277-CCEG, 2010. As of August 18, 2014: http://www.rand.org/pubs/conf_proceedings/CF277.html

———, *For Whom the Whistle Blows: Advancing Corporate Compliance and Integrity Efforts in the Era of Dodd-Frank*, Santa Monica, Calif.: RAND Corporation, CF-290-CCEG, 2011. As of August 18, 2014: http://www.rand.org/pubs/conf_proceedings/CF290.html

———, *Corporate Culture and Ethical Leadership Under the Federal Sentencing Guidelines: What Should Boards, Management, and Policymakers Do Now?* Santa Monica, Calif.: RAND Corporation, CF-305-CCEG, 2012. As of August 18, 2014: http://www.rand.org/pubs/conf_proceedings/CF305.html

———, *Culture, Compliance, and the C-Suite: How Executives, Boards, and Policymakers Can Better Safeguard Against Misconduct at the Top*, Santa Monica, Calif.: RAND Corporation, CF-316-CCEG, 2013. As of August 18, 2014: http://www.rand.org/pubs/conf_proceedings/CF316.html